Sexual Issues with Children

Promoting Healthy Rather than Unhealthy Behavior

Dave Ziegler, Ph.D.
Executive Director
Jasper Mountain
Jasper, Oregon

Jasper Mountain
37875 Jasper-Lowell Road
Jasper, OR 97438-9704

E-Mail: davez@jaspermountain.org
Website: www.jaspermountain.org

Cover Design: Rachel Bakke
Cover Photo: ShutterStock and Michelle Perin

International Standard Book Number: 978-1507641095

This book is dedicated to

young people who have been initiated into sexuality in the

worst of ways

and who deserve to learn the beauty and the wonder

of a sexually healthy life.

May they all find the teachers they so

truly deserve.

Acknowledgments

Much of what I will cover in this book comes from my work with the sexually abused children of Jasper Mountain, an organization designed to give hope to the most damaged children and the families who try to help them. Any large scale project requires a team effort, and Jasper Mountain is both a large scale project and a remarkable example of teamwork. The organization's goal is to make a significant impact on the lives of very damaged children to the degree that they will have a chance at both a successful and fulfilling life ahead of them. What makes this lofty sounding goal the challenge that it is comes from the place we must start with every child in our program. Early traumatic experiences including child abuse, chaotic living environments, and serious neglect have set in motion a cascade of serious problems for the children Jasper Mountain is designed to help. It takes a great many people with unique skills to meet our goal to help these difficult but deserving children, and the best news is how well Jasper Mountain is succeeding.

As skilled and committed are the people who make Jasper Mountain successful, they are also individuals who know that they get so much back in return for the work they do. That is the true magic of Jasper Mountain, where everyone wins — the children, their families, the staff, the Board and supporters and the community as a whole. From the terrible reality that there is child abuse comes the possibility of an organization like Jasper Mountain. I want to thank everyone involved with Jasper Mountain, the Board of Directors, the staff, the volunteers, the individuals and businesses who support its work, and most of all the children who share their pain, their promise and their lives with us. The Jasper Mountain Board of Directors consists of Rob Morris, Steve Cole, Gary Buss, Cathy Ouellette, Kerrie McIntyre, Parke Blundon, Nji

Nnamani, Debra Eisert, Barb Lucas, Randy Nawalaniec, Chuck Davis, Gene Heinle and Nathan Lichvarcik. Without this excellent Board of committed individuals there would be no organization and no success stories.

I also want to thank my wife Joyce who works harder than anyone to make a difference for our children. Thanks to Judy Littlebury, Michelle Perin, and John Ziegler who helped edit the drafts and offered very helpful suggestions.

I am grateful to Mac Hindman for giving permission to reprint the "10 Commandments of Healthy Sexual Behavior" written by Jan Hindman. Also to Wendy Maltz for permission to include aspects of her CERTS Model of healthy sexuality.

I want to thank the staff of BluePrint Studios of Melbourne, Australia for their contribution to our work. Starting in 2009 Reuben Street decided to make a documentary of the work being done at Jasper Mountain so this story of hope could be told on an international scale. The result of four years of work including four trips from Australia to the United States to capture the story on film is the documentary 'Once Upon a Mountain.' This full length film premiered first in Melbourne to a capacity crowd and then premiered in the United States with an even larger capacity audience in December of 2013. The film distinguished itself with both its story and how the story is presented by winning the Best Documentary Social Benefit Award at the Eugene International Film Festival in 2013. It will now become available for general distribution. The commitment to this project including the hard work and all expenses involved was a labor of love for Reuben Street, his wife Rima Darwiche and his film crew of John Di Flumeri, Elio Rulli and Freya Fullwood. The story of hope that is Jasper Mountain will now be told far and wide thanks to the impressive dedication and skill of these wonderful people.

Their efforts to spread the message of hope for all children will make a difference now and in the future. I am most grateful for their contribution to our work.

Finally, I want to thank my former professor and mentor on issues such as healthy sexuality. Dr. Sandy Mazen has been an inspiration in my life to think critically and live fully. An expert in human sexuality, Sandy has been a supervisor, business partner but most of all a life-long friend. He has enriched my life, for which I am very grateful.

Contents

Preface

This is the second of a series of books covering topics that parents, teachers and therapists struggle with every day in their attempts to help difficult children. The first volume, in what has been called "The Success Series," covers attachment. First things first, why call this "The Success Series"? It is understood that any adult who has the challenge of working with a difficult child will want to succeed in this endeavor. But before going into the success for the adult, let us start at the beginning and first consider success for the child.

It may seem odd to hear this, but regardless of what you are running into with the child you are working with, the child is currently succeeding, however it is very possible that you are not. Of course, the measure of success for the child is different than it is for the adult. We adults want our children to be successful in social settings and school, developing and keeping true friends, giving and receiving support in the family, and overall reflecting positive emotions that are consistent with living a happy life. However, that is not the measure of success to the difficult child. It may be a bit different for every child, but I have noticed the themes are the same. The child believes he or she wins when the adult loses. Adults lose when they get angry, frustrated and make statements about giving up. Where we want them to fit in well, they want to set themselves apart; we want them to laugh and enjoy life, and they prefer to yell and disrupt any calm they find with a good tantrum. In other words, difficult children consider themselves a success when they succeed at what we would consider failing. This is the second of several excursions into the thinking of disturbed children that we will take together in this series; the first was Attachment: The Social Foundation of a Successful Life.

The reason success for the disturbed child is measured by failure is complicated, but, simply stated, it is because in the perception of the child what adults consider success is out of reach. There have been dozens, no thousands, of experiences where an adult has made it clear the child will likely never reach the top of the success mountain. The climb is difficult for any child, but what child will attempt to make the journey if he or she has been convinced that the result will simply be more failure? So what I am pointing out is that most adults miss the forest for the trees; they do not see how hard disturbed children work to succeed by their own definition.

I stopped telling these children long ago to work harder because they were just not putting in enough effort. Take a closer look, they may be working harder than anyone to continue to disrupt, to tantrum, to make it clear to any and all adults that they are unlikely to fit into the mold we want them to fit. Consider how much energy it takes to throw a respectable tantrum. Do you remember the last time you 'threw a wobbly' (Australian for tantrum)--not just getting upset, but a fit that registered on the Richter Scale? This would usually mean real anger, some yelling perhaps, even slamming a door or throwing something. Now remember how tiring this was. Difficult children can do this several times a day (some several times an hour), and that takes a lot out of a person. But these children have years of training in preparation for the Olympic Tantrum Team, as soon as it becomes a competitive sport. I realize I am making light of something very serious to most adults, and I am doing so on purpose. Regardless of our challenges in life, if we cannot take an occasional step back to laugh at our situation and ourselves, then the issue has become greater than our ability to manage it. When this happens our internal confidence hits dangerously low levels, and we fall into a state some describe as "burnout."

But my point in starting with how successful disturbed children consider themselves is that most of these children have not given up; they try much harder than adults give them credit. Many have all the makings of a champion, but the drive and energy just goes in the wrong direction. So I am suggesting we start from a place where we see the child as very committed, hard-working, persistent, and a tireless champion at failing in most areas that we consider success. But we must recognize this fact because we will want to redirect this Herculean effort they are investing in their lives. To insure that most of us are on the same page, if you have a depressed, sullen child who does little or nothing, I would still include these children in the self-defined success camp. It is not a natural state for children to expend little external energy, sit in dark rooms and brood. Look at the effort it takes to fight the natural instinct to be interested in the world around them. But these children, whom I call the internalizers (as opposed to the externalizers), must be worked with differently and can be more challenging than the aggressive and violent children.

So consider that we do not have a child who is a failure, we have a child who is succeeding in all the wrong things. It may take some time before we help the child's brain realize that there is another way to succeed that brings even greater benefits.

Now we can return to the concept of success for adults. We started with some insight that the children I have lived with for decades have taught me that disturbed children do care and do put in considerable effort, and this realization is the start of success for adults. This is because you will not succeed with a disturbed child unless you understand the child, which includes their inner world of contradictory thoughts and feelings.

We adults have a bad habit of measuring our parenting success by how well our children perform on the measures we define as important. For example, the parent of a straight "A" student may have a bumper sticker on their car that appears to acknowledge the child, but before the child is mentioned it says "I am the proud parent of..." Who is really being recognized? Such parents often take pride in their skilled parenting even when their motivated and bright child asks for little academic assistance. However, the parent, who night after night works with the math-impaired child (an impairment to which I can personally relate) only to see a "C" on the report card may struggle wondering if they are giving the child enough. I believe it is important to give credit where it is due, and I do not let busy professional parents off the hook just because their child does fine with little help. I also do not hold the parent of a struggling child responsible when the parent is working hard to help, despite the outcome.

We must start this Success Series with the understanding that to do our best is the best we can do. Therefore, success as a parent is what we do and not what our child does. But let us add to our definition of success to improve our outcomes in preparing a child to have the potential at a future with social connections, with personal goals that are set and accomplished, and with a degree of personal contentment along the way.

We will cover a variety of topics in this Success Series, and each will add to the overall plan. These books will be short and to the point and are not intended to be exhaustive of the topic. If one of the topics is of great interest, then look into that topic more because there are many helpful resources. Before this series I rejected the notion of a book on a specific topic because the children I am writing about essentially never have just one problem area. My previous books have been about the whole child, although this theme will be continued in this series, there will be more attention given to a specific topic. I still believe that success will only come from treating the total child, and this means addressing multiple problem areas. If you have completed one or more parts of the "Success Series" and you find them helpful, then I suggest you consider reading some of my more comprehensive books that have a broader focus on the child. If you have not run into these books, they are:

Raising Children Who Refuse To Be Raised – This book takes a disarmingly frank approach to the most difficult behaviors and the most challenging children. It not only explains the causes of the most serious problems parents face, but it goes further to provide interventions that have been tried and found successful. Very serious problems such as aggressive, violent, explosive, hyperactive and belligerent behaviors are addressed in a practical and understandable way. Sections of the book are geared directly to parents and other sections to professionals with a suggestion that everyone read both, so adults are working closely together to help these children.

Achieving Success With Impossible Children - Written for those who work with children who are the most troubled and challenging, and who are exceptions to all the rules. It offers practical applications and hands-on suggestions to help children become healthy successful individuals. Clearly written and infused with humor, it discusses working with difficult children in multiple settings such as during adoptions, in schools, with parents, and in residential care. It provides advanced intervention ideas including positive discipline and teaching responsibility. The message of the book is that success with very challenging children is not only possible, but realistically achievable.

Traumatic Experience And The Brain, A Handbook For Understanding And Treating Those Traumatized As Children, Second Edition - This volume details the effects of childhood trauma on the developing brain and describes how early events in life rewire the person's perceptions of self, others and the world. It incorporates two decades of research on the human brain and answers the question, "So now what?" Now that we know a great deal more about how the brain works and how it is affected by trauma, what should we do differently to help traumatized individuals? Case examples help explain in understandable terms how we must work with the human brain and not work against it.

Beyond Healing: The Path To Personal Contentment After Trauma – This book takes a close, critical look at many of our beliefs about human limitations and offers a message of hope for those individuals who have paid such a high price for past abuse and trauma. Drawing on case studies, it provides a clear and realistic guide to reclaiming one's life after traumatizing experiences. The hope offered is based upon science and research and the writing style is accessible and down-to-earth. This book can be an invaluable guide to anyone who has personally experienced trauma or is attempting to help someone who has.

Neurological Reparative Therapy, A Roadmap To Healing, Resiliency And Well-Being - This book provides a new model of treatment that integrates critically important components of brain functioning. This new integrated model is first brain focused (neurological) and stresses the healing (reparative) of adverse impacts that have prevented the brain from reaching its potential, and outlines a roadmap of an active process (therapy) in promoting healing, resiliency and overall well-being. The NRT model relies heavily on the research and professional literature of: brain development, trauma, attachment, and resiliency. The NRT roadmap identifies the best route to well-being through healthy brain development, attachment, and resiliency but relies on the helper to use his or her own skills, experience and techniques to take the journey.

Attachment: The Social Foundation of a Successful Life – The first in The Success Series. No single issue points to success in life as much as the ability to bond with others. Life itself depends upon the ability of a baby to connect with a source of safety, nourishment, and emotional support. But many children do not find the world they are born into a place where their basic needs are met, and they form barriers to connection that can be life-long impediments to success and happiness. This book describes in technical and practical terms what can go wrong in the development of attachment in children and what to do about it. Helping a child to bond and attach to others, despite the vulnerability this entails, may be the single most important step any parent or professional can take to improve the life of a child.

I have only one goal for all of the above books – to help you succeed in working with difficult children and to learn from the journey. I have been blessed in my personal life and my professional career to have the very best of teachers, and I want to share what I have learned with you. So let us begin our journey with the starting point of remembering these basic things:

- Disturbed children are highly motivated to succeed in being a failure.
- We must measure our success not by what the child does, but by what we do.
- Our own success will be linked with how well we understand the inner world of the child's thoughts and emotions.
- If we lose our sense of humor at any point in the journey, then parenting a difficult child will simply be a burden, and this will put us on the road to burnout and failure.

Before we begin the journey I want you to know that you can do this; you can be successful with your difficult child. You may be saying, "How can he say this and mean it, he doesn't know me or my child!" Please consider that I do mean this, and I have worked with and lived with thousands of difficult children, many of whom would surpass your child for the future Olympic Tantrum Team. I have also worked with thousands of adults, from those with extensive experience to those with no experience at all, and helped them to be more successful. We know from psychology that two things help reduce the stress of a difficult challenge (and parenting a disturbed child is at the top of the difficult list). The first is having a plan of attack, and I will help you with this. The second is having confidence; if you lack confidence in yourself, for the time being, accept my confidence in you. Now put aside your worry and your stress, and apply your energy to fully understanding the problems, and then come up with a plan that will improve your success at helping the children we will be discussing.

Dave Ziegler

Introduction

How healthy are you when it comes to your sexuality? This is not likely a question you have ever been asked or even asked yourself and, if you have, you have probably found that it is not an easy question to answer. The word healthy has traditionally been linked closely with our bodies or physical health. Being physically healthy is important for sexual health, but certainly not the only factor. How healthy are your sexual attitudes, your sexual thoughts, and your sexual behaviors? Like other aspects of living, there is no benchmark to compare your sexual health to a 'one size fits all' standard. One of the main reasons for this is the influence of culture, values, mores and beliefs. Few issues are as culturally determined as sexuality. What is acceptable in one culture may be forbidden and abhorrent in another culture.

I began our review of sexuality with the question of health because few topics are as complex as sexuality, and when it comes to teaching children about sexuality, we need to know what our destination is in order to know how to get to where we are going. Often sexual themes are put in the context of normal and abnormal. Although normal sexuality will be discussed, I do not find it sufficiently helpful to determine our goal with children. Instead, I am proposing that we consider what is healthy and unhealthy rather than what is normal and abnormal. As we will discuss in Part I, what may be quite normal in our American culture cannot always be considered even remotely healthy from an objective point of view.

Sexuality is one of the most complex dimensions of a person's personality and very self. Our sense of who we are as a person begins with our sexual orientation. How we view ourselves determines how we relate to others. We learn from our culture what is acceptable and what is not. When conflict arises between who we are and what our society expects us to be, this may determine the amount of stress we live with. Our very perceptions of our self are to a significant degree determined by our sexuality. The world of perceptions we live in determines the world we experience. Whether it is thoughts, feelings or behavior, sexuality is inescapable for us all. Unfortunately, the influence of sexuality on our lives is not always positive and affirming. For many, sexuality brings guilt, secrecy, and not only stress, but torment.

How does one live a healthy sexual life? Who are the role models available for healthy sexuality? We can all name some "sex symbols," which even within this term is the suggestion of an object rather than a person, so this can't be healthy. Magazines come out with the annual "sexiest person alive," only to surprise and confuse the very individuals who find themselves on the list. Does the quantity of sexual experiences count? If so, Wilt Chamberlain's claim of 12,000 partners would stand out, as would Hugh Hefner's lifestyle, but he stopped counting when he hit his 80s. But many would not consider either of these individuals a model of healthy sexuality. On the other end of the continuum there are those who attempt to live in a way to transcend sexual pleasure for 'a higher level of being.' Such a stance is often expected of spiritual teachers. But is avoiding sexuality a healthy path? The search for role models of healthy sexuality is likely to end in frustration because, from the start, our sexuality is very personal and individual. How someone can live a life that is sexually healthy may come down to understanding one's own private beliefs and rules of behavior, and then living consistently within this internal moral framework. If this points us in the direction of health, then the roadmap to healthy sexuality requires a very individualized and introspective journey. However, few individuals are prepared to take this journey and arrive at their destination without help along the way.

This book will strive to help you be a guide (perhaps after deepening your own sexuality) for young people who don't know which way to turn and often hear 'if it feels good then go the other direction because it can't be good for you.' To all the judgmental and self-righteous individuals and institutions that see sex as the worst aspect of a human being, we must stand up and say, "sex is not only good but great; it is not only one of the highest forms of human communication but the only way we can join in divine creation itself." But before we reach the highest aspirations of sexual health we must begin at the most fundamental level, and the starting point is a personal look inward at ourselves.

Dave Ziegler

Author's Note

Every parent must face the issue of sex when raising a child. The lucky parents are those with children who seem unaware or uninterested in sex throughout childhood. But even for these parents the time comes when the question should be asked, "But is it normal that my child isn't even curious?" There is no way around the issue. A common attempt to sidestep the issue of teaching healthy sexuality is to take the position, "They can ask me what they want to know." These parents don't seem to remember that for most children there are many preferable (and more interesting) sources of sexual information than a parent. Ignoring the topic of sex until you can't avoid it is not the most healthy strategy, it essentially means you will let someone else teach your child about issues related to sexuality. Many adults grew up with parents who did this and should know there are better ways. But like preparing your income taxes, you may have put it off because there is always something you would rather do. One major difference is there is no deadline to teach healthy sexuality, and how many people would get around to paying the IRS if there was no April 15th deadline?

The issue of developing healthy sexuality and then teaching it to someone else is one of life's truly great challenges. What is even more difficult is to teach healthy sexuality to a child who has experienced sexual abuse. As you will learn in this book, our culture is just beginning to ask how to promote a healthy perception of sexuality after sexual abuse, as demonstrated by a complete absence of information on this topic. That's right – no books, no specific training programs, and few experts anywhere. But millions of parents are raising children who have experienced sexual molestation, and without help these children embark on a lifelong struggle with sex. These children deserve better, and the parents who have the challenge to raise them deserve some help. This is my motivation to write this book. So why take your time to read this? I will offer two answers to this question, and both are related.

First, I have attempted to provide two facets to each issue throughout the book, a detailed description as well as a practical explanation. The practical is the more important because if this effort is successful, you will receive specific tools to help both the child and you. If I provide an in-depth analysis without providing you with ideas on how to address the problem, the usefulness to you is diminished. I will supply suggestions along the way that may also include a few brief stories to help make the point.

Second, my credentials on the topic of sexuality have not come in the classrooms of graduate schools. It is true I have had professional training in many aspects of sexuality such as couple's therapy, treatment of sexual dysfunction, and sex education. But I have had to learn about healthy and unhealthy sexuality primarily by four decades of working with children with sexual issues. I have been a therapist and psychologist for over 40 years, and for most of that time I have lived with some of the most challenging children in the United States. As a health psychologist it has been my responsibility to help children learn healthy ways to live, and sexuality has been an important topic. Before I could teach the children, I had to look at myself, consider the hurdles involved, and consider how to help on his issue. I want to offer to you what I have learned, and perhaps some of my thoughts will be of help.

As I say in all my books, your time is valuable and I respect your need to make the best use of it. Therefore, pick any section of this book and read a couple pages to see if you want to take the time to read the rest. If you are in a situation where you need some questions answered quickly, you might consider looking at the Table of Contents and go to that section. If you have an immediate issue you might also consider reading Part III first and then return to the first two parts. In whatever order you read this book, it is my hope that I can convey to you what I have learned from the children I have worked with to assist you in facing your own set of challenges. If that is not the case, contact me and let me know.

Part I: The Impact of Sexuality in the Life of an Individual

This entire book could focus on the impact of sexuality on a person because sexuality influences a person's identity, personality, behavior, communication style, dress, spirituality, personal traits, and so much more. The complexity of sexuality cannot be overstated because this life-affirming part of every human being is at the same time the source of some of life's most persistent confusion and anxiety. Most people have conflicting views about sex – both their own sexuality and that of others. Nations have conflicting views of sex as well. An example of this is on the day I wrote this the second most populous country in the world (India) announced that homosexual acts are illegal. And this is in a country that has a significant homosexual population where gay lifestyles are overtly practiced and the laws against homosexual sex are not enforced. It seems the Indian people are more comfortable with these laws in place for symbolic reasons than not having them, but the Indian people also do not expect these laws to be enforced. This sounds somewhat similar to America's 'don't ask and don't tell' policy on gays in the military that went on for many years, we knew better but just did not know what to do. More will be said on American culture later.

Most public issues are the acceptable topic of discussion, but for the most part, a serious discussion on sexuality is not appropriate in polite company. No other topic arouses (an intentional use of the word) as much disdain, judgment and fascinated interest as sex. It is a part of our biological and psychological makeup. It is a significant part of our economy and business practices such as marketing. Sex is how the human race survives as well as thrives. It is entertainment, it is crime, it is spiritual practice, and it is the essence of love itself. Sex is a lot to get one's head around; is it any wonder that sex draws a great deal of attention in everyone's life.

Starting in childhood we are curious and interested in sex, but we learn it is not a topic for children. Is it good or bad, beautiful or disgusting? When we are children we are interested in sex and want to know more. For most people this stance toward sex does not change a great deal throughout life, at least in the American culture. Few individuals in our culture were lucky enough to grow up in a family where sex was considered an integrated, healthy part of life, meaning it was no more and no less important than other aspects of individuals and society. Children start off curious about many things, including sex, and if their curiosity is addressed they move on to other topics of interest. But children soon learn that some topics are secretive and, of course, that makes them 'the forbidden fruit' and they get even more interested. Like the story of the Garden of Eden and the forbidden fruit of the tree of the knowledge of good and evil, tell a child not ever to go into a particular room in the house and guess what they want to do at the first opportunity? Few children get their curiosity sufficiently addressed during childhood, and the result is often a life-long approach/avoidance struggle with sex. Children learn sex is taboo and forbidden and they are supposed to look away, but have trouble doing so. This could be a metaphor for our culture when it comes to our attitudes regarding sex, where our societal values around sex are not obvious in how we act.

Most people grow up in a sexual vacuum; our bodies physically develop long before our higher reasoning centers mature to the degree that sexuality can be understood or appreciated on a thoughtful level. This appears to be one example of how Mother Nature seems to have gotten it wrong. Physical maturation of sexual organs allows for child bearing when women are young and healthy. On a physical level this makes sense. However, the sexual organs that mature early are not the most important sex organ; the brain has this distinction because it can facilitate understanding, self-control and good decisions around sexual behavior. This appears to come from our membership in the animal kingdom. Clearly the early ability to reproduce makes more sense with other parts of the animal kingdom than it does for human beings. But an undeveloped brain combined with a fully developed reproductive system can produce very poor sexual decisions, as we all learn either from experience or observation. The result of poor reproductive decisions can include criminal acts, sexually transmitted diseases and teen pregnancy, and with children raising children usually in conditions of poverty. Without a brain's higher order reasoning center developed at the point of high sexual interest, what is needed to avert tragedy are clear cultural mores with rules, boundaries and supervision—all of which are lacking for teens in our society. Since the "sexual revolution" of the 1960s and 70s (if not before), the result has been decades of struggle with high rates of teen pregnancy, only one of many societal problems surrounding sexuality in America.

It seems to be a universal experience for most of us to feel that when it comes to sex everyone else seems to know more than we do. Why is that? Perhaps it is the utter complexity of sex. There are facts and information pertaining to sex, but there are also direct experiences. Some sexual experiences can be very uncomfortable and awkward. All positive sexual intimacy requires great vulnerability, but with vulnerability often comes self-doubt. As adults in America, we are bombarded with the message that sexual attraction is very important and it is likely that everyone else is more sexually active and satisfied than you. Sexual behavior as portrayed in advertising and the media is nearly a contact sport with proficiency ratings, but how do I match up with the norm or at least with what my partner(s) expect? Under these conditions, how do each of us manage to develop a healthy sexuality and then pass this on to our children?

All cultures have rules around sex and most of the rules are prohibitions. Most are designed to put some control on the individual. We not only have prohibitions on sexual behavior, but also what we look at and even what we think about. At least in the American culture, the prohibitions do not seem to be successful when it comes to controlling people. Like so many other aspects of growing up, many of our attitudes and perceptions are formed early in life and persist into adulthood. The complexity of sex, along with the fascination and lack of sufficient information in childhood, all combine to produce high interest and high confusion—both hallmarks of conflicts around sex in our society.

The signs of our cultural conflict with sex are everywhere. For example, there are few topics that raise more energy in school than sex education. Parents don't fill the school board meetings with protests about how to teach about wars, crime, or even genocide. Violence they will say is simply a part of life. But somehow educators teaching children about sex is different and steps over some invisible line for these parents. Our culture's professed high standards around sexual behavior are not consistent with the enormous amount of money generated by the sex industry that quietly includes many major corporations. Nor are these standards reflected in the number of sex crimes. In the news today was the arrest of a top aide of a family values conservative congressman for violation of federal laws on child pornography. Both the aide and congressman were instrumental in drafting legislation on child pornography laws the aide is accused of violating. There is a long list of politicians, preachers and 'pillars of the community' who say one thing and do the opposite related to sexual values. The individual examples of sexual hypocrisy in our society seem endless, from self-righteous conservative ministers to politicians including illicit sexual behavior in the oval office of the White House. Cultural conflict around sex is only one of many factors that makes the job of raising a sexually healthy child one of the most difficult jobs for parents.

What is Sexual Health?

Most every parent knows that healthy sexuality is much more than all the 'thou shalt not' prohibitions. So what is healthy sexuality? In part it must include physical health. This includes how our own body works and ensuring steps are taken to promote vigor and prevent illness. Healthy sexuality is understanding emotional connections with others and how human touch is a significant communication tool. It is knowing how love can be enhanced by sex and how love can be damaged by sex as well. It is understanding what is expected of us by our culture and social conventions, both what we choose to follow and what we choose not to follow and the potential consequences. Healthy sexuality is knowing our own values and boundaries and adhering to them. It is having positive thoughts, positive emotions, and allowing a place in our lives for physical and sexual pleasure. Sexual health requires some level of the spiritual dimension sex can bring to a relationship.

The World Health Organization has considered the many components of sexuality and has stated, "Sexuality is complex: it includes gender roles and sexual orientation and is influenced by the interaction of the biological, psychological, cognitive, social, political, cultural, ethical, legal, historical, religious and spiritual factors" (WHO, 2006). As complex as sexuality is, how do all these areas fit with health? Again, the World Health Organization presents its definition of sexual health, "Sexual health requires a positive and respectful approach to sexuality and sexual relationships, as well as the possibility of pleasurable and safe sexual experiences, free of coercion, discrimination and violence" (WHO, 2010).

Another definition of healthy sexuality is the conscious, positive expression of our sexual energy in ways that enhance self-esteem, physical health, and emotional relationship. It is mutually beneficial and harms no one (Maltz, 2014). This definition appears to be focused on adults, but there are important components that fit for children as well, such as: enhancing the self, it must not be physically or emotionally unhealthy and does not cause harm.

Other writers have attempted to take the complex concept of sexual health and break it down into its main areas. The Minnesota Department of Health identifies seven components of healthy sexuality in adults, and they will be mentioned here because healthy adults begin their journey to health as children.

- Communication - interaction with others in productive ways around sexuality.
- Relationships - develop friendships, partnerships with healthy boundaries.
- Self-Esteem and Self-Worth - enjoy sensual and sexual feelings, nurturing self and others.
- Education - understanding and valuing the role of sexuality in self and others.
- Values - having and living by a personal code and respecting this in others.
- Body integrity and protection - safe and healthy sexual activity.
- Spirituality - appreciating the sacred dimension of sexual connection and its role in bringing together body and soul (Hadsall, 2010).

Psychologist and sex educator Patrick Carnes breaks down sexual health into 12 areas.

1. Nurturing - capacity to receive care from others and care for oneself.
2. Sensuality - awareness of physical senses that creates emotional, spiritual, and physical presence.
3. Self-image - positive self-perception that includes embracing your sexual self.
4. Self-definition - clear knowledge of both your positives and negatives, and ability to express boundaries as well as needs.
5. Comfort - capacity to feel at ease with yourself and others about sexual matters.
6. Knowledge - about sex in general and your own unique sexual patterns.
7. Relationship - capacity to enjoy intimacy and friendship with friends of both genders.
8. Partnership - ability to maintain a relationship that's intimate and erotic, and interdependent but equal.
9. Non-genital sex - ability to express erotic desire emotionally and physically, without using your genitals
10. Genital sex - ability to express erotic feelings freely.
11. Spirituality - ability to connect sexual desire and expression to the meaning of life.
12. Passion - capacity to express deeply held, meaningful feelings of desire about one's sexual self and intimate relationships (Carnes, 1997).

Sexual health is a pervasive concept, but it must also be a highly personal one as well. In a sense, everyone must find what sexual health means on a personal level. What may work for others may not be healthy for me. Values, beliefs, and boundaries are all highly personal issues. So there is no way to approach sexual health without becoming highly personal and giving consideration to the many areas within a person, as well as the factors all around the person in the immediate environment and larger culture. Violating cultural or legal prohibitions regarding sex can have serious consequences at times, and therefore culture must come into our discussion. There are places in the world where the same sexual behavior is acceptable in one country and a crime punishable by death in another. While we may not choose to follow all sexual conventions in our environment, we need to know what our social situation expects of us and what we may face if we chose to ignore or openly reject standards of behavior.

While acknowledging the substantially complex components involved in sexual health, a practical definition of sexual health will be offered here. Sexual health is understanding one's own personal values, beliefs and boundaries in regard to all aspects of sexuality and living in harmony within them. Regardless of whether you use this or your own definition of sexual health, if you wish to help a young person achieve sexual health there are a number of obstacles our society puts in the way.

Perhaps the Most Unhealthy Sexual Culture on the Planet

It is easy to find ratings on many issues internationally from education, longevity, income, child mortality and many other topics. However, you will not find a rating of countries measuring sexual health. Therefore, the following statement is my own position and not one established by the World Health Organization or any other legitimate authority. Our American culture is perhaps the most unhealthy culture on the planet when it comes to sex. Sex is everywhere in our culture, but not in a healthy context. Sex sells and is a profit-making tool in many aspects of our economy. A few examples include the use of sexual themes to sell products, promoting movies and television programs and, long before any other industry was able to do so, pornography was the only internet-based business to be profitable and hugely so.

Pornography, or more accurately the sex industry, is yet another indicator of how unhealthy our culture is. For this discussion we will set aside the thorny problem of defining pornography (other than Chief Justice Potter Stewart's infamous statement that he may not be able to define it but, "I know it when I see it"). Short of a small percentage of 'liberated' individuals who admit that they are consumers and enjoy sexually explicit materials, our expressed societal values do not match our behavior. Some may wonder who actually views pornography. The answer turns out to be a very large number of people around the planet, led by Americans. Hollywood puts out many films, and in some years an average of one film a day is released in this lucrative industry. However, in a recent year there were 50 adult films released for every film of all other genres. One thing can be counted on; if no one is watching and no money is being made by sexually explicit films, then the steady stream of sex films would not be what it currently is. In fact, the most lucrative movie of all time is an explicit sex film. There are many people who would never enter a sex shop, which by the way in America outnumber all Starbucks and McDonalds stores combined, but routinely view sexually explicit material at home or in their respectable 4-star hotel rooms. In fact, an estimated 70% of room service profits in the hotel industry come from adult materials provided in rooms. Although they don't advertise it, major hotel chains such as Hilton, Marriot, Holiday Inn, Hyatt, Best Western, Choice Hotels, and Sheraton, to name a few, are all involved and bringing in important financial profits through the sex industry.

It is not just the 'hospitality' industry that is involved in making money from sex. Other major corporations making huge profits on explicit sex include: AT&T, Comcast, General Motors, eBay, CVS Pharmacy, Barnes and Noble, 7-Eleven, Yahoo, Time Warner, Amazon, Frys, Conoco and the list could continue and fill this page. In fact, it is practically impossible to financially invest in a balanced portfolio and specify that no part of the investment can be connected to the sex industry.

The dirty secret of the American mainstream corporations getting their share of the profits of the sex industry is not much of a secret anymore; it is simply considered smart business. A final fact on the sex industry and financial profits is it turns out that as obsessed as the American culture is with sports, the profits from all sports in America do not come close to what the sex industry brings in every year in financial return. Considering the millions of people contributing to profits from sports, how many more millions must be contributing to profits from the sex industry? Clearly our stated values do not match our behavior in American culture, and one definition of sexual health is to have clear values and then live in harmony with those values. But there are other troubling issues that must be considered when parents are trying to raise healthy children in an unhealthy society.

Nudity Sells

It is not just movies that promote nudity. Three recent cable television programs appear to attract viewers by putting nudity in their titles and in the show. Naked Vegas, Naked and Afraid, and Buying Naked are all recent shows in the naked reality genre. Actually the shows are about art, survival and buying houses and are much more tame than their titles. But how else can TV producers make buying a house in Florida sound sexy?

Perhaps the next concerning dynamic traces its roots back to the Puritan settlements of New England. This influence within the American culture does its best to demonize sex and the result, perhaps intentional, is to make it more alluring. This was not the goal of the Puritans but may be the goal of many in our American culture. If sexuality were simply considered a part of everyday life, it would be much less interesting than we make it in our culture. We prohibit sex, we make a great many laws to control it, we establish standards of "decency" and then we violate all of these prohibitions. The result is an unhealthy fixation on sex rather than healthy interest and acceptance of this aspect of every person. The intentionality primarily comes from the economic potential of sex. If we are fixated as a culture, then sex can be used to sell any number of products and services. If we were more sexually healthy, the predictable result would be less attention given to the use of sex to promote economic gain. There is less intentionality with this lack of congruity between our values and our behavior when it comes to laws and morality. But when moral and legal limits are placed on normative behavior, the end result is a loss in respect for our institutional guidelines and a loss of sexual health.

One of the most telling aspects of our lack of sexual health concerns nudity. Few cultures have as much nudity accessible in so many forms as does our society. Depictions of sexual behavior are provided in most aspects of our entertainment industry. Any facet of sexual proclivity can be found instantly on the internet. One of the allures to pornography is how it pushes the limits, but if anything goes and everything is accessible, just how does it continue to shock and exploit limits? In recent decades the answer has been to move from gratuitous and sexualized nudity to any and all types of sexual behavior, and finally the new frontier of humiliation, violence and linking sex with pain. Whereas nudity could

11

have been shocking a hundred years ago, now the shock value is mostly gone short of the half time of the Super Bowl. Sexualized nudity is everywhere, and although still considered taboo in most areas of our culture, it has become so common place as to have lost much of its allure, but not entirely. In the context of an unhealthy sexual culture, how is a parent to raise a child with a healthy acceptance of their own body and at some point sharing intimate behavior with another?

There are many challenges but the final one I will mention that adds to the difficult job of a parent to raise a sexually healthy child in an unhealthy culture has to do with how sexuality and sexual behavior are presented in the media. According to movie ratings, the depiction of enormous amounts of violence are considered more acceptable for children to view than certain anatomical parts of either a male or female. But the economics of restrictions in the media goes back to the Garden of Eden--where the prohibited forbidden fruit makes it more desirable. Films add sex scenes and nudity to increase profits as they do with violence and profanity. What may work well for the bottom line of a film does not work out that well with the message our culture sends to its young people.

What material is not suitable for young people to view?

The Motion Picture Association of America voluntarily self monitors content in films to avoid external monitoring. The MPAA rating system purports to determine what material is suitable for children. However, one of the industry's most popular films in 2012 was not restricted from children with a rating merely suggesting parental guidance. The film's story line was repeated depictions of children intentionally killing other children. Perhaps Hollywood did not find children murdering children objectionable, but where was the public outcry? This is one of many stunning examples of our culture's perverse values when it comes to the message we give our children.

There are multiple unhealthy messages in our media related to sex, including but not limited to: sex is dirty and therefore desirable, nudity objectifies women as well as men, certain body characteristics make someone more or less sexy, a person's value is in their physical attributes, being desirable requires adherence to strict physical and behavioral standards, and many more. Since 99% of people do not have the bodies or desirability of the most recent media sex symbols, then how is everyone else to make peace with being less than the standard? Most well- adjusted adults would simply laugh at falling short when compared to a Hollywood sex symbol, but developing teens are another matter entirely. Here is where the complexity of sex enters the situation. To develop healthy sexuality a person must have acceptance of personal physical and psychological traits. Therefore our culture not only does not help in the job of developing healthy sexuality with our young people, it is intentionally antithetical to sexual health in many ways.

Countering Societal Influences

To raise a sexually healthy child you must be prepared to go against the many ways that our society uses and perverts sex. You must be willing to be 'old fashioned' or 'out of step' in the eyes of your child. The individuals who use sex to sell products and entice interests are not considering what a young person needs to be sexually healthy, but you do need to consider this. Our society will not make this difficult job any easier, so be prepared to go against the flow of a society that does not follow its own stated sexual values.

Physical Impacts of Sexuality

Sex is hugely influential on our physical bodies. From before birth our bodies are developing sexual definition that will determine much about who we are throughout life. At birth our society puts us in one category or the other — male or female. However, science has known for some time that nature is not as black and white with a sexual dichotomy as is commonly believed. Our culture is well aware that some males and some females are attracted to their same sex. Gay marriage is currently a hot cultural topic with even the conservative state of Utah currently issuing marriage licenses to same sex couples. By the way, in another cultural contradiction the conservative State of Utah, to the surprise of many, leads the nation in the consumption of pornography (Edelman, 2009).

Identifying children as discretely one gender or the other is complicated for a number of reasons. I will not go into all the permutations of ambiguous sex identification, but here are just a few issues. We know that some males prefer to live life as females, and some females live as males. Some adults of both sexes go through extensive surgeries for sexual reassignment. In most of these cases the individual has a self-perception of being the opposite sex and that nature somehow got it wrong. But sexual identification is not just an issue with adults. Some children at birth have undifferentiated sex organs, others have sex organs not consistent with their male/female chromosomes. Some children have both sex organs and some children appear to lack genitalia. This is a very complex topic and an overview of this issue can be found in the TED talks titled "Is anatomy destiny?" (Dreger, 2011) and Ambiguous Sex'or Ambivalent Medicine? (Dreger, 1998). The lifelong work of psychologist John Money also goes into this topic in great detail (Money, 1996). So at times rather than identifying sex genitalia at birth, a sex is assigned to a child and consideration is given to surgically making sex specific alterations. If you think these permutations of gender are rare oddities, then think again. The day I am writing this a new law goes into effect that allows individuals in America's most populous state, California, to use the restrooms according to how they define their own gender and not necessarily what it says on their birth certificate. The cover story of Time Magazine addresses this topic in the article "The Transgender Tipping Point" which reports that Facebook now identifies no fewer than 50 choices when indicating gender. Transgender individuals account for several of these 50 choices, and Time reports that there are more than 1.5 million people in the United States who identify with the term transgender (Steinmetz, 2014).

The International Olympic Committee has a serious problem with gender determination and they do not have a workable answer. The challenge is to insure fair competition among males and females. Specifically the IOC must insure that a male does not compete in the Olympics masquerading as a female. The simplistic and unworkable solution the IOC announced within the last year was to check hormone levels among athletes. More scientific consideration should have taken place because hormones will not provide a reliable means of sex typing. Even if a better scientific test was used with chromosomes, this too may in some cases be faulty. The reality is that there is no known medical or scientific test to definitively put someone in the dichotomous categories of either male or female. It turns out that nature is much more comfortable with ambiguity than our culture is. It can therefore be said that in the big picture it is not nature but often culture that determines our assignment of gender. I stress this point to show how important the educational process is. If we can determine the sexual identify of an individual by what they are told and how they are raised, it is clear how important education is to how sexually healthy a young person can become.

Based upon the male or female category we are in, our families and our society expect us to fit into a range of gender specific traits. Whether fair or not, or enlightened or not, little boys are enculturated and taught differently than little girls. There are some boys and girls who rebel or fight these pressures, but for the most part males and females conform to our culture's expectations based on their sex.

Although upsetting to some who would like the sexes viewed the same, most boys are quite different than girls in physical, hormonal and neurological ways. The norm for males is to have more weight and muscle mass, heavier bone structure and slower overall development than is the norm for girls. The brains of girls actually function differently in some ways than boys. There are ways our bodies form around the expectations our society places on our gender. In other ways our personalities are influenced by our bodies. But either way, sex is a major contributor to who we grow up to become as a person.

There is a reason why on most information forms we are asked our name, age and sex, almost always in that order. Our name is a handle to identify us, but our age and sex are the two most important influences in who we are. Our sex will heavily influence our body type, our risk tolerance, our vulnerability to diseases, and even our longevity. Based upon these differences, historically people pay more or less to get insurance of all types based upon their sex.

Very recent news accounts have put a spotlight on the physical differences in males and females. A controversy began with research done on a popular medication to improve sleep with the brand name Ambien. A study found that long after the drug was released it was found that males and females assimilate the drug very differently (Farkas, Unger & Temple, 2013). The conclusion of the study indicated that, in general, females needed half the therapeutic dose of Ambien needed by males. One serious finding of this study was that some females in the morning still had a high level of the drug in their system potentially causing impairment in activities such as driving a vehicle. This was only the start of concern about medication trials. A closer look at the issue of physical sex differences in prescription medications has now identified a major flaw in how they are researched and tested. Previously the belief was that males were the best subjects of clinical research due to the lack of hormonal factors in females that might compromise the findings. Using males not only included humans but also laboratory animals such as mice. If males and females respond very differently to prescription medications, the primary use of males in trials may well have produced significantly faulty results. If this highly precise field of medical science did not understand sex differences in males and females until very recently, then how many other parts of our society have made the same error thinking that males and females are basically the same on a physical level?

There are specific ways that nature and nurture play a role in the influences of sex on our bodies. Nature provides us with genetic loading with predetermined values for intelligence, size, eye color, body shape and sex. Nurture steps in to provide texture for how we physically develop, how we feel about our physical self and how we use our physical characteristics. Nature and nurture must combine to produce who we are psychologically and physically. Every possible permutation can be found through these two influences. Genetics for large body size can be severely impacted by early serious neglect. Genetics for very high cognitive level can be devastated by fetal alcohol syndrome. A genetic female may be enculturated to have male physical traits, and genetic males may be raised to have female traits in their physical and psychological make-up. How a child is raised to view their own sexuality can play a major role in both physical and emotional qualities they develop.

> # Children must understand male and female perspectives
>
> Sexual equality among genders is a foundation of sexual health. The sexes are different but they have more in common than they have differences. Raise your child to understand and respect different perspectives. In that way we can do what nature does and bring Mars (male) and Venus (female) into the same gender solar system of sexual harmony.

Emotional Impacts of Sexuality

It can be a type of chicken and egg conundrum when considering whether our brains produce hormones because of our gender or if our gender is determined by our hormones. It is somewhere in between. But the influence of sex on our body directly impacts our emotions. We have cultural stereotypes that females are more emotional and 'big boys don't cry,' but such sex traits are taught rather than biologically determined. But science has found there are gender differences in both thoughts and emotions (Else-Quest, Hyde, Shibley, Goldsmith & Van Hulle, 2006), and these differences have been found across cultures and socio-economic status (Underwood, Moore & Galperin, 2002). Other research points out that separating nature and nurture with the impact of sex on emotional disposition is not conclusive (Coie & Jacobs, 1993).

Perhaps the best approach to determining if sex has a significant influence on emotions that are not culturally influenced is to look within the brain for differences. When this has been done, sex differences have been found in how the brain is optimized to generate emotions (Ingalhalikar et al., 2013; Beltz, Blakemore, & Berenbaum, 2013). But perhaps it is an academic exercise to try to separate sex from cultural or influences of the environment (nurture) since no one is culture free and we all develop our emotional dispositions from nature and nurture.

But sex does not just determine how we internally process emotions, it is also a major influence in how others relate to us and what expectations they have around emotional expression. If we present emotional dispositions contrary to what might be expected for our gender, others may perceive this as concerning and may result in interpersonal distance. Males in the work place may be passed over for promotions if they demonstrate stereotypical female patterns of emotional expression. On the other hand, females that express culturally determined male expression may be considered cold and aloof and viewed with suspicion. Aggressive girls in elementary school may be viewed with concern as might passive males. Children learn very quickly how they are expected to express feelings and this is one reason that nurture is such a strong determinate in the influence of our gender and our emotions.

Sex is a major factor in our personality and in how we present ourselves. Like snowflakes, there are as many personality types as there are people and sex is a determining factor in all of them. We communicate to others who we are by our character traits that are a major aspect of emotional expression. We may relate to others with culturally male or female emotional traits or we may go against the mold, but either way sex is an important influence.

How we handle stress is affected by sex. Once again it is difficult to determine how much is nature and how much nurture, but undoubtedly both are involved in how we handle stress. Both males and females have the same internal stress response cycle but the results can look quite different. The stress response cycle is how the brain identifies environmental threat in the hippocampus, relaying information to the pituitary and adrenal glands to produce glucocoidicoids and activating the emergency fight or flight response. There are few differences in this cycle based upon sex but significant outcome differences. Females much more often exhibit the flight response, which can look like running away or psychological flight such as freezing, dissociating or fainting. On the other hand, males much more often show fight responses. However these differences also are influenced by age and experience in the world. Younger children of both genders more often use flight and dissociation due primarily to their perceived inability to fight off a threat successfully. Therefore, the most powerless individuals turn out to be young females, and faced with serious or chronic threats these children can develop debilitating internalizing flight responses such as: dissociation, fainting, chronic anxiety, self-harm, eating disorders and levels of depression.

As individuals age and mature, sex plays an important role in physical as well as emotional development. Our physical size is to a significant degree genetically determined. Gene expression and sex hormones impact our physical size and shape. Gene expression often determines the onset of puberty and the significant hormonal release causing the range of physical characteristics related to sexual maturation. Although males and females have the same hormones, they do not share the same amount of these hormones. A higher amount of female hormones will produce female physical and emotional characteristics in the developing individual as will higher amounts of male hormones with male characteristics. Some of these differences include physical size, muscle mass, bone development and voice tone. Emotional differences can also be impacted by the amount of male or female hormonal release.

If raising children through the developmental periods of life is not complex enough, the role sex can play compounds the complications. For a child to be sexually healthy, we must have at least a general understanding of the factors that influence the development of the child and sex is one of these important factors.

Spirituality and Sex

It is often said that a holistic view of a person must include mind, body and spirit. Before considering how sex is related to one's spirit, a few comments on our spiritual dimension are in order. The word spirit has many meanings but all are related. A person is said to have spirit, a thoroughbred may be spirited, a school may have team spirit, all are related to energy and enthusiasm. There is also the spirit world or the Great Spirit, meaning a dimension beyond the material world. At death the life spirit of a person leaves them and this meaning of spirit combines energy with another dimension. Spirituality is both the spark within a person as well as a connection to a dimension beyond the material world. It is both belief and perhaps faith, it is an orientation to existence and meaning and it is a sense of connection to something greater than ourselves.

For some individuals spirituality is the cornerstone of their life; for others spirituality is the source of reactivity and negative stress. The difference comes back to health. Briefly stated, the suggestion here is that spiritual health is much the same as sexual health; we have values and rules to live by and we adhere to our own rules if we are healthy. When people react to spirituality they are often focused more on religion or more precisely the religion of their upbringing. For many people early involvement in a religion and its doctrine have provided a helpful foundation for their life, but there are many others who struggle with, reject or have ongoing anger over their enculturation with religion. Healthy spirituality requires an internal investment and practice within a belief system rather than a reactivity to what others believe or practice. If something is healthy for the individual it must be helpful and not harmful, whether it be spirituality or sexuality.

There are many similarities to these two types of health— spirituality and sexuality. They both provide models for understanding our self and both offer guidelines for behavior, particularly in relationships with others. Spirituality is most often viewed as our highest self. Sexuality on the other hand is split between our most primitive nature on one hand and our highest nature on the other. Humans are animals and nowhere is this more apparent than in our sex drives. Most people do their best to control their sexual appetites, but this battle for control demonstrates the most fundamental of conflicts within humans who are at once animals and also capable of high levels of spiritual attainment. To be truest to our nature and to be whole and achieve optimal health, we must embrace our animal and our spiritual natures. Sex can be one of the best expressions of this balance of the dual nature we possess. This is a central factor in the potential of sexual behavior to be one of the most profound experiences of a person's life and at other times one of the lowest levels a person can descend to. Sexual expression has the potential of being sordid or profound; the difference comes down to what we make it.

In most spiritual traditions the act of love making has the potential of procreation. In other words, sexual intercourse can be an opportunity to join with the divine to create new life and new spirit. In many traditions this is the most specific example of humans exercising their highest nature by being a part of divine creation. However, sexual intercourse motivated by negative intent can be one of the most base and degrading acts a person can carry out. The conflicts of values, rules and our split natures are most apparent in sexual contact with another person. The same behavioral act can either be one of the most heinous crimes—rape, or one of the most valued acts—intimate love making. What separates the two to a large extent is consent, motivation and level of respect involved. All three of these issues come back to spiritual boundaries and rules. Therefore if sexual behavior is devoid of spiritual health then it is much more likely to reflect our primitive selfish nature. The potential of sex to be repugnant or resplendent is not lost on those who seek profit from selling sex. Turning something potentially beautiful into something perverse is one way the sex industry draws attention.

These brief comments about spirituality and its importance to sexual health reflect the holistic necessity to not teach sexual health as an isolated aspect of a person. As stated above, health has mind, body and spirit components. Sexual health also has mind, body and spirit components. The importance of including each along with the critical concepts of consent and respect in educating a young person to be sexually healthy will be a major theme of Part III.

We Give to Our Children Our Healthy or Unhealthy Sexuality

With the goal of helping a child become sexually healthy, and particularly trying to do so in what arguably is a sexually unhealthy culture, we must look at who is to teach them. An honest look at where children learn about sexuality will end up with some concerning sources of information. In modern America how sex is presented in the media is a major source of children learning about sex. The influence of peers may be nearly as important a source, but it is difficult to separate the media and peers because all children are influenced by what is going on around them, particularly influences that will hold high credibility to a developing young person. Media influences will certainly include movies, television, music, books, magazines and the lives of teen idols in all these areas. A relatively recent influence is the animated but very lifelike video game industry.

As parents, if we stop and think about it, we must admit that sexual attitudes are learned from the media and the world presented to our children, but we all want to say that our children will learn from better sources of sexual information such as family, school and church/synagogue. But how good of a job do these preferred sources of sexual enculturation do? Although values and moral codes are a central part of any religion, it is doubtful that a religious organization would consider itself a primary source of sexual information. Our schools may manage to provide text book sexual information, mostly from a biological perspective, that is unless there is major local resistance to sex education. Few school districts would pride themselves as giving students a comprehensive understanding of sexuality that would go well beyond biology to include the three cornerstones of healthy sexual behavior – consent, respect and motivation.

Regardless of what many parents would prefer, the answer to where a child must learn about healthy sexuality is from the parent. When I say the parent I am including everyone who is in the role of parenting, including foster parents, mentors and staff in residential treatment settings. Much like religious and academic institutions, few parents would say they are prepared to fulfill this role much less believe they are doing the job now and doing it well. Ironically, the only sources of information on sex that have no hesitation in reflecting any and all sexual content are precisely the sources that do the poorest job—the media. To be fair, the sources of video, audio and print media do not see that it is their job to teach children healthy sexuality; their job is to: attract attention, entertain, sell product and universally to make money. One thing sexual content has always been successful at is as a source of making money. In producing some of the most questionable reflections of sexuality, media sources will say that it is the job of the parent to screen content to which they want their children exposed. In this way they believe they are relieved of responsibility. However, parental screening or censorship is not the same today as it has been in the past. With the universal use of mobile devices that play most anything, anytime and anywhere, how is a parent to know what a young person is viewing or listening to, and how feasible is it for them to exercise any control other than set guidelines they expect the young person to follow? As never before we may have arrived at a place with our technology that the genie is out of the bottle when it comes to accessing sexual content, and it appears it will stay that way.

Regardless of where we may look to find the needed source of instruction in healthy sexuality, we find that we must arrive back at home—the only truly workable source of information on sexual health is the guidance and instruction of an involved parent. This may not be the most enjoyable job of a parent but there is no way out of this responsibility. A parent need not attend classes in sexual biology at a medical school, be an expert on psychology and interpersonal communication, or obtain a doctorate in sociology to understand the mores of sexuality in our culture. Being a guide to sexual health is first of all to know what it is, then take advantage of some quality information from trusted sources, some of which will be offered in this book. But ultimately the strongest influence a parent will have is to model sexual health. As we discuss this challenging role of a parent, one thing we may all agree upon is that, like other pursuits, the teacher ends up to be the one who learns the most.

Being comfortable addressing sexual themes is important and few of us find ourselves naturally at ease with the topic. It may take work to become comfortable and this work begins with a look at our own upbringing regarding sexuality. A consistent theme with adults is to raise their children similar to their own upbringing. This default mode is often subconscious. At times we raise our own children almost the opposite to our own upbringing. For example, if we had a repressive and strict father, we might be a permissive and flexible parent. Or if we struggled with being forced to practice a religion as a child we might give our own children a choice in whether to attend a church. If we had a family in which there were few traditions or rituals, we may raise our own children with more structure and family observances. But whether we parent in a similar or intentionally dissimilar way, our own upbringing is a major influence in our parenting.

When you were growing up, how was sexuality handled in your home? What was the spoken message about sexuality and what was unspoken? Were your parents a helpful source of information or were all sexual themes on the list of taboo subjects? In the trainings I have given, I have often shared one impactful chapter of my own sex education. I was fourteen at the time and I had a brother a few years older and a brother a year younger. My father was a career officer in the Air Force and when I was a teen he often had the same approach to commanding a unit of soldiers and parenting his kids. After all his sons became adults, his aloof rule based approach changed radically to a highly personable and supportive friend. But back then he was "Sir." One evening he called the three of us together and said in a confident voice that each of us was to meet him in the family room after dinner. Before dinner we looked at each other and asked, "Did you do something? I don't think I did." And then my older brother said this might be "The Talk" but did not elaborate. I thought throughout dinner what the talk might be about. I was to find out quick enough.

When we were seated in the family room my father walked in and said he expected complete attention because we were going to learn about sex. I looked at my older brother and he mouthed "I told you so" without saying a word. I was actually ready for the lesson and wondered how my father would handle this topic that was not characteristic of him to bring up. The way he handled it was to reach into a briefcase and pull out an LP record and put it on the phonograph and he stood looking at us as the record began. I must admit I was rather disappointed in the lack of detail on side one of the record. For the next 15 minutes I heard about how plants and animals reproduce and how seeds and eggs were involved. As the record moved up the animal kingdom and got to how humans reproduce, there was a pause and reference to side two of the record. At this point my father asked if there were any questions so far, as I remember there were no questions since how fruit trees are pollinated and how snakes normally lay eggs did not generate a great deal of further inquiry. But I knew that side two was where the action was and it might bring up some questions. At this point my father ordered me and my younger brother to go do our homework, but my older brother was to stay and hear side two about humans. "No fair," I thought, but in our family you didn't say something like that to my father. Later I asked my older brother to fill me in and he dismissed me by saying, "When you grow up."

The rest of this story involves first the fact that my father never in the subsequent years called me or my younger brother into the family room to hear side two. Perhaps that is one factor behind my interest throughout my career in sexuality and perhaps a factor in writing this book in that I have had to search on my own without the benefit of side two of the sex education record. As an adult I recalled this incident when I was studying sex therapy in graduate school and I asked my parents about the event. We had a good laugh at the fact that my mother told my dad that he was to take care of this subject because that is what fathers do with their sons. My dad had no idea what to do and even less interest in the task so he went to the library and checked out a record on sex education so he could tell my mother that he had done his part.

As a marriage counselor and psychologist I have heard from many people over the years how they received instruction in sex at home. Some were better than my experience, but many missed out even on side one! For those of us that received little useful and informative understanding of sex from our parents, it may be helpful to consider where we learned our information and what attitudes we learned about sex while growing up other than it was not for kids, it involved shame and guilt, and it must be terribly special to have everyone so guarded about it. Once we remember how and what we learned it is important that we consider how we will do the educating differently, because without some consideration, our default might be to give our children what we received, in many cases no direct education on sexuality at home. By the way I was never able to find and listen to side two of the record, but something tells me as a psychologist and sex educator it would have provided more amusement than practical information. So at this point you may want to reconsider reading further from a book written by someone who never listened to side two!

Regardless of how you learned about sex and sexuality, before trying to pass on sexual health to a young person, it may be helpful to consider your present beliefs, attitudes, and personal sexual health. Since sexuality is so complex with domains that include biology, physiology, psychology and more, perhaps a good way to start an internal assessment of your own sexual health is to answer some questions. The following is an unscientific but practical questionnaire about your sexual health.

Sexual Health Questionnaire
Dave Ziegler, Ph.D.

Sexual health is much more than behavior; it includes attitudes, perceptions, emotions, beliefs and personal orientation. This questionnaire addresses the broadest meaning of sexuality. Answer the following as accurately as possible; don't answer as you think you should but rather with your most honest response. Each item has a scale to choose the best number on the continuum provided in each question. *Be aware the scale (10-0 and 0-10) changes with the items,* so pick the best number for each question.

1. Sexuality has brought life-long enjoyment to me--Sexuality has brought me guilt shame and stress.

    10   9   8   7   6   5   4   3   2   1   0

2. I am comfortable looking at or touching my body--I am embarrassed by my body.

    10   9   8   7   6   5   4   3   2   1   0

3. I accept sexual beliefs and behaviors of other people even if they are different than mine--there should be one sexual code for everyone.

    10   9   8   7   6   5   4   3   2   1   0

4. I treat my body with care and respect--I should be more careful and respectful to my body.

    10   9   8   7   6   5   4   3   2   1   0

5. I don't know what I believe about sex--I have well developed beliefs and attitudes about sex.

    0   1   2   3   4   5   6   7   8   9   10

6. Sexual intimacy has been a very negative part of my life--it has enhanced my life.

    0   1   2   3   4   5   6   7   8   9   10

7. I appreciate and enjoy sexual feelings--sexual feelings are wrong and must be avoided.

    10   9   8   7   6   5   4   3   2   1   0

8. I feel guilt and remorse about sexual decisions I have made--I always make good decisions about sex.

    0   1   2   3   4   5   6   7   8   9   10

9. I have healthy sexual thoughts--I have sexual thoughts that are disturbing.

    10   9   8   7   6   5   4   3   2   1   0

10. Sex is private and I find depictions of sex disgusting--I can read or watch depictions of sexual behavior without discomfort.

0   1   2   3   4   5   6   7   8   9   10

11. I can be nurturing and loving to another person with or without being sexually intimate--I'm not the nurturing type, I like to be nurtured.

10   9   8   7   6   5   4   3   2   1   0

12. I enjoy or at least can participate in serious discussions about sex--I am very uncomfortable and dislike talking about sex.

10   9   8   7   6   5   4   3   2   1   0

13. I avoid being vulnerable to people I am close to--I am able to be vulnerable with another person.

0   1   2   3   4   5   6   7   8   9   10

14. I seldom consider the other person's feelings regarding sex--I understand the importance of respect in sexuality.

0   1   2   3   4   5   6   7   8   9   10

15. I do not follow my own values--My sex life reflects my values.

0   1   2   3   4   5   6   7   8   9   10

16. I expect others to respect my boundaries and I respect the boundaries of others--I often feel guilty due to my sexual behavior.

    10   9   8   7   6   5   4   3   2   1   0

17. I enjoy being intimate with a partner--Intimacy is stressful and I avoid it or am glad when it is over.

    10   9   8   7   6   5   4   3   2   1   0

18. I do not have sexual health--I consider myself sexually healthy.

    0   1   2   3   4   5   6   7   8   9   10

19. I am aware of the risks involved in sexual behavior--I do not consider myself at all knowledgeable about sexual risks.

    10   9   8   7   6   5   4   3   2   1   0

20. Sex has improved my relationships—Sex has brought conflict, stress and mostly unhappiness in my relationships.

    10   9   8   7   6   5   4   3   2   1   0

21. Sex is fundamentally selfish and is about meeting personal needs--Sexual behavior and communication is always a two way street.

    0   1   2   3   4   5   6   7   8   9   10

22. I am comfortable with my knowledge and understanding of sexual matters--I feel ignorant when it comes to information about sex.

    10   9   8   7   6   5   4   3   2   1   0

23. With sexuality I understand the role of rights, respect and responsibility--I don't have clear ideas on the role of sexual issues in relationships.

    10   9   8   7   6   5   4   3   2   1   0

24. If the other person does not want to be sexual it is that person's job to stop it, not mine--I am clear about the role of mutual consent in sexual behavior.

    0   1   2   3   4   5   6   7   8   9   10

25. I am very comfortable with my sex life--I am troubled and/or dissatisfied with my sex life.

    10   9   8   7   6   5   4   3   2   1   0

Final Self Check—How honest have you been in this questionnaire?

This question is critically important. If you have been less than completely honest with yourself, than the results are of little value. Therefore when you are ready to take a completely honest look at yourself, than complete the questionnaire again before scoring the results.

Scoring

The most important question is how you feel about the results, not a score. However, as a point of reference the total score reflects the following:

0 – 100   Poor overall sexual health. It will be difficult to help guide someone else to sexual health starting from here. Self-reflection and making changes in many areas could produce improvement.

101 – 150   Fair sexual health. A score in this range may reflect a low priority for sexuality and improved health could be the result of more attention to this area as well as being a better guide and teacher to a young person.

151 – 199   Good sexual health. You are likely satisfied with the role sex plays in your life, but there are opportunities to increase the benefits sex can offer you. Keep in mind that modeling is the most powerful teaching tool when helping a young person develop sexual health.

200 – 250   Excellent sexual health. Sexuality is making a positive contribution to your life. You present an excellent role model for others in this area, but you may want to consider direct ways to instruct young people on being sexually healthy; teaching can bring additional challenges, but you are likely motivated to meet them.

Few of us were raised in an open and sexually enlightened environment with parents who were models of sexual health. For example, what would your parents score on the above questionnaire? Consideration of how we were raised to understand sex is not about looking for blame but what we must now do to bring more health to this important part of each of us. What are the areas we are uncomfortable with or avoid? We cannot and undoubtedly don't want to change how we view sexuality, but there may be certain areas where we wish to grow and bring our attitudes and behaviors in better alignment with our beliefs. If so, the inventory above may point to some areas where you want to improve. It is nearly universal that sex produces discomfort and anxiety as we go from childhood to teen years to our adult years. There are actually good reasons why this important; very private and complex topics cause stress, but why should this be the case indefinitely? With desire and effort, sex can become simply what it is—a wonderful aspect of our human nature and our emotional and psychological makeup. This moves us toward the healthy sexuality that we want for the young people we parent and help.

A good starting place to become more sexually healthy is to learn to discuss sex and sexuality. Many adults experience stress when they attempt to either initiate or respond to sexual themes with children or teens. Most individuals are more comfortable discussing a topic in which they are very knowledgeable, and adults believe they should know all about sex. They think how embarrassing it would be to be asked a question about sex and not know the answer. The fact is that sexuality is so complex no one knows the answers to all the questions that come up. We may find more comfort being honest about not knowing some aspects of sexuality with other adults we trust. Here is a good place to begin to develop more comfort by bringing up conversations on sex with an adult friend or partner. Gauge your comfort level in initiating such a conversation and do the same after you have had several discussions. Mere repetition can often significantly increase someone's comfort level. Another good exercise is to practice admitting that you don't know some details about sex and consider how to obtain the information.

Parenting is considered one of life's most difficult tasks. Being an effective parent and preparing a child to live a full and healthy life is even more difficult, then add to this challenge imparting to a child a healthy sexuality in a culture with few good role models and continually representing examples of unhealthy sexuality. The point is not to say this task is impossible, but knowing the difficulty can help you see that preparation, personal support, and gaining confidence will all help you succeed.

Is all this work really necessary? After all, didn't most of us have poor sexual education and we made it? Although each of us may have "made it," how much better could our sexual lives have been if we were welcomed into a sexually healthy world and learned to internalize a sense of pleasure, closeness and wonder at what sex can offer a person over the lifespan? What a gift we are able to offer a young person! But it is not just for others that we can learn more about sexual health. It may well be that as the teacher we can learn the most in this process. So in your quest to offer sexual health to a young person, be open to becoming a more sexually healthy person yourself and perhaps everyone will gain in the long run.

Summary Points

➢ Sex is integral to our lives, our culture and even our economy, but for the most part it stays in the background and is seldom addressed in an honest, direct and healthy manner.

➢ Most children are interested in sex, but usually what they learn is what they are not supposed to do with their sexuality.

➢ The American culture has a confused and erratic stance toward sex that does not promote healthy sexuality. Our culture makes it harder to promote sexual health.

➢ Sex is a major influence in our physical development, our emotions, our personality, and who we become as individuals.

➢ Male and female are not opposites, and we all have parts of both within us from physical hormones to psychological traits.

➢ Sex is so fundamental to who we are that it is integral to our spiritual health.

➢ It is unavoidable, we give to our children our own healthy or unhealthy sexuality. If we want our children to be healthy, it is our responsibility to be healthy ourselves.

➢ For the sake of the child, make a commitment to be sexually healthy yourself and everyone will come out ahead.

Part II: Abnormal or Unhealthy Sexual Behavior

A frequent question asked of professionals by parents is whether their child's behavior is normal. Like the dichotomy of either male or female, most people think there must be a clear distinction between normal and abnormal. But as we briefly discussed in Part I, male and female are not black and white distinctions, and normal and abnormal are even less distinct. Normal behavior can cover a continuum of behavior. In statistics, a typical normal distribution can be represented by a bell shaped curve. Most of the distribution congregates around the mean or average. However, a normal distribution also moves further from the higher frequencies and tails off in both directions from more frequent to less frequent. In a similar fashion normal behavior is on a continuum. Most of the behavior congregates in the middle or average, but less frequent behavior is still within the norm and therefore the question becomes how infrequent must a behavior be to not be normal? While it is understandable that parents want to know if behavior is normal, this actually gives us very little useful information, and there are reasons to say this is the wrong question. The question of normal sexual behavior is much more of an academic question that what most parents are really asking, which much of the time is closer to, "How do I discourage inappropriate sexual behavior or behavior I do not want and am not comfortable with?"

Normal vs. Abnormal or Healthy vs. Unhealthy

The word normal has many meanings, but in the context of sexual behavior it means that the behavior or issue in question fits into a norm or a pattern that is expected and conforms to a regular pattern. Another way of saying normal would be an average and fitting within an expected range. However, if a behavior is expected then there is someone who is doing the expecting. If it fits a norm, who sets the norm? Normal is established in the context of the environment. What is normal or expected in one setting would be abnormal in another. For example, loud and boisterous behavior would be normal at an athletic event but abnormal in most church services. It is the context of sexual behavior that is the determining factor, just because behavior is taking place frequently and is expected does not mean it is either desirable or healthy. The Department of Transportation keeps detailed statistics on accident rates by age group among drivers. It is an expected pattern to find the highest rates of automobile accidents occurring with teenage drivers, therefore, it is the norm or normal. But this expected pattern is neither desirable nor healthy. Similarly, to determine what is normal sexual behavior does not reflect whether the normal behavior is desirable or healthy. Although normal behavior will not be the primary focus for developing interventions coming up in Part III, it is worth taking a look at normal behavior in children.

What Is Normal When It Comes to Sex?

Even if determining what is normal sexual behavior is not the best question, it is a starting place. Many adults are actually surprised to learn some of the behaviors that are normative, meaning an expected behavior that is not unusual, among children. Here are a few examples:

Preschool children:
- Like to be nude
- Want to watch others use the toilet
- They attempt to touch the private parts of peers and adults
- They put objects in body orifices

Elementary age:

- Gravitate to 'dirty' words for body parts and sex
- Play doctor and inspect private parts of others
- Are fascinated with urination and defecation
- Expose themselves
- Draw genitals on figures
- Like to see others nude
- Pretend to be the other gender
- Initiate looking at and touching genitals of peers

(Cavanagh Johnson, 2013).

If some of these same behaviors came from a teenager or adult they would be crimes (penetration with a foreign object, exhibitionism in public, and voyeurism). However, with young children all these behaviors are actually not unusual and therefore within the norm or 'normal.' This helps point out that although a behavior may be normative or normal, it can still be unwanted and not be appropriate behavior.

Jan Hindman, a friend and experienced sex educator who died at a young age, was fond of telling audiences that when many adults find children exhibiting sexual behavior their faces would turn purple from discomfort (Hindman, 1985). She would go on to say that in such situations an adult finding a child self stimulating or masturbating might without thinking say something like, "Stop that, don't touch yourself there, it is icky and dirty, save it for the future to share with someone you love!" Few parents who gave it some thought would knowingly make such a ridiculous statement, but Jan's point is adults need to give some consideration to the messages they send the child when reacting or overreacting to a child engaged in normal sexual behavior.

Since humans are a member of the animal kingdom, then sexual behavior can be a factor at any age. Nature intends for sex to stimulate nerve centers often producing pleasure. It is not only normal but natural and healthy for an individual to pursue pleasure and avoid pain. All animals have instincts, and sexuality is influenced by instincts. Considering each of these factors, what is normal or normative for children can actually involve a wide range of interests and behaviors.

The Role Sexual Behavior Plays for Children

One of the many binds for parents is what to do about sexual behavior in general. Much, if not most, child sexual behavior is unwanted by parents and other adults. For example, normative sexual behaviors are not tolerated in schools, day care centers, public swimming pools, church youth groups, team sports, summer camps, shopping malls, essentially all community settings and in most family homes. Children are therefore sexual beings with little if any acceptable way to be sexual. What we teach our children is to repress most sexual interests and even sexual thoughts, except for the occasional question about where babies come from. Although children seldom have permission for any sexual behavior, most do not seek permission, and thus most children will exhibit sexual behavior in some form as they mature. Most sexual behaviors create a problem for parents because the behavior is not wanted and the child is often told it is wrong or inappropriate. But when prohibitions are not successful at extinguishing the unwanted behavior, it can then be challenging for a parent to determine if certain sexual behaviors or interests go beyond annoyance and should be of more serious concern.

Many adults are reactive and confused by the sexual behavior displayed by children. The goal is to avoid reactivity, understand the behavior and respond in the most healthy and effective way possible. Understanding childhood sexual behavior is not as complex or confusing as it may seem.

Sexual behavior can play a number of roles for children, and to understand a specific sexual incident it is helpful to consider what the child's behavior is communicating. This is also true for adults. Adults look to sexual behavior to meet their basic need for touch, express closeness, feel good, express love and affection, reduce stress, get reassurance, and many other positive motivations. However, sex can be much less positive when used to dominate another, express power and control, or to use or abuse another person without consent in the process of meeting personal needs without regard to the needs of the other person. In the same way, sex can communicate many messages in adults, this can also be said for children. Children also have both positive and negative motivations with sexual behavior and only your clear, non-reactive thinking is going to help you decide in this situation what the sexual behavior means.

Understanding the meaning of sexual behavior

Start with a clear head, if the behavior you run into has upset you, calm down before you try to understand it. It often is helpful to think through the behavior with another adult who can help with a non-reactive perspective. Consider several possible options, then use your best judgment from knowing the child. Do your best to consider what happened, why it happened and what was the child's motivation. It often helps to discuss the incident with the child as you read the child's energy. You may not always be right in your assessment, but you don't have to prove anything in court; you simply need to do your best to find the most probable explanation of the incident to know how to best respond.

A frequent theme in the psychologist's office is to have a distraught parent talking about finding a child doing something sexual. There are any number of variations on the theme of concerning sexual behaviors. For example, a parent of a young child might find two siblings 'playing doctor' and exploring body differences, or a child inserting objects in their own anus or another child's. A parent may find a hidden cache of underwear ads or even nude pictures from a magazine. Or a parent may come across diary entries with real or imagined descriptions of sexual acts or drawings of anatomically correct figures perhaps engaged in sexual contact. Any of these discoveries can be anxiety producing and can raise questions in the minds of some parents if there is a sexual problem with their child. Clearly some issues regarding sex are normative and others should be of concern to the parent, but how does the parent tell the difference?

Healthy and Unhealthy Behavior, Telling the Difference

It has already been pointed out that because some behavior is normal or not unusual does not make it acceptable or wanted in your home. And just because a large number of children (or adults) in our society exhibit a behavior does not mean it is healthy. There are two helpful tools to distinguish behaviors that need some special attention from those that may need simply more supervision.

The first is primarily for very young children. It is a small 26 page booklet written by Dr. Toni Cavanagh Johnson. Dr. Johnson has spent her professional career working with children and their parents, and sexual issues are one of the specialties she has pursued. Her booklet is titled *Understanding Children's Sexual Behaviors, What's Natural and Healthy* (Cavanagh Johnson, 2013). This resource provides helpful information regarding the prevalence of sexual behavior in children, for example, adults in one research study recalled solitary (82%) and mutual (76%) sexual behavior with other children. The booklet also identifies 20 characteristics of problematic sexual behaviors in children. The booklet distinguishes three categories of sexual behaviors from

"Natural and Healthy" to "Of Concern" to "Seek Professional Help." The booklet is designed to address sexual behavior of children up to the 4th grade. *Understanding Children's Sexual Behaviors, What's Natural and Healthy* can be purchased from the website http://www.tcavjohn.com/ for $2.50.

The second tool is the Inappropriate Sexual Behavior Scale (ISBS) (Ziegler, 1987). The background of this scale goes back more than twenty years. At the time I was directing our treatment center for children who commonly acted out sexually. I received a call one day from the local Child Protective Services office to attend a meeting concerning an unknown topic. When I arrived, there was a long table behind which nine State administrators sat and in front of them a chair for me. It felt a bit like the Inquisition. I was asked to explain why there was a high rate of sexual molestation that was going on in the program I ran. Since I was unaware of any sexual molestation that had occurred in our program, I was surprised by the question. I listened with part amusement and part irritation as a couple dozen incidents were read aloud that had been compiled by caseworkers of children in our program over a number of years. A few incidents included: a young child in a game tagged another on the buttock, another child touched a child in a private area while swimming under the water, two children 'exposed' themselves while putting on swimsuits at a public pool, and so on. All of the children involved had been previously sexually abused and all were placed in our program by the very people questioning me because they could not be put into foster homes due in part to sexual behavior.

I had been working with sexually reactive children since the early seventies and when I expressed surprise that they used the term "molestation" for common normative and sexually reactive behavior, I was told, "If a child is touched in a private area regardless of by whom, we consider it molestation."

Coming from the legally responsible authority to determine what sexual abuse was, I found this both ignorant and shocking. I decided to either find or develop a tool that could distinguish normative behavior from molestation or pathological behavior. Since I was unable to find a tool in 1986, I took the time to research and develop one, and the result was the ISBS.

The ISBS acknowledges that behaviors are unwanted and inappropriate but the question is whether the behaviors are either abuse or characteristic of pathology. The scale identified five categories of behavior, looks at the attitudinal state of the child at the time (this can make a major difference), and can identify a reportable incident of abuse. Unlike what the State administrators said in my meeting, just because a child is touched in a private area of their body does not equal molestation; it depends on many issues such as who, how, when and why. No doubt in the decades since there is a more sophisticated understanding of childhood sexual behavior among the administrators in that meeting or those who now have this responsibility.

Parents aren't the only ones who react to sexual behavior

Don't feel badly if you have found yourself surprised, flustered and at loose ends when facing sexual behavior in children. You are not the only parent to do so, and it is also not just parents who overreact. I did not expect to find the people who carry out the laws determining acceptable sexual behavior to be as out of touch as the story above, but they were nonetheless. Overreacting to childhood sexual behavior can be found with police officers, mental health professionals, the clergy and even in the courtroom. Handling sexual situations well takes work and some practice, but it is an important part of being a good parent.

The five categories of sexual behavior include the following-- starting with normative behaviors and with each category reflecting more concern:

1. Sexualized Expression - writing, drawings, language and masturbation
2. Cooperative Sexualized Expression - mutual sex games of exploration
3. Emotional Abuse of a Sexual Nature - exhibitionism, voyeurism, obscene calls
4. Emotionally Coercive Sexual Abuse - premeditated genital contact with manipulation and thinking errors
5. Physically Coercive Sexual Abuse - forcible demeaning or physically hurtful sexual abuse

In addition to the facts of what happened, the motivation and attitudinal state of the child is also an important component in determining the significance of the child's behavior. The ISBS considers the motives and energy of the child under each of the five categories. This scale has been used since it was developed to successfully understand the sexual behavior of children and aid in an appropriate and effective response, rather than a reactive and panicked response. You can find the Inappropriate Sexual Behavior Scale in the appendix of this book.

The two assessment tools are offered here to help consider sexual behavior and its meaning and importance. Adults can make mistakes on both ends by overreacting to sexual themes with children or underreacting to sexual issues. Family values must come into the discussion with sexual behavior. What your family values are regarding sex is your decision. That is why both scales consider behavior on its own, and you will have to determine what is and is not acceptable in your home.

But with the help of these tools it may help you have a balanced and thoughtful response to sexual behavior, which is not easy to do.

Unwanted Sexual Behavior

Just because a behavior may be 'normal' or even healthy does not mean that you want to either encourage or tolerate the behavior in certain settings. You need to be aware that children are sexual beings and will reflect sexual interests and curiosities. But establishing boundaries of acceptable behavior are important, and as a parent it is your job to be clear with your child as to what is acceptable and unacceptable. Because this can at times be complex, put the unwanted behavior in the context of family rules rather than moral rules or right and wrong. It can be difficult to grow up believing a behavior is morally wrong, but this all changes on your wedding night.

What Makes Sexual Behavior Unhealthy?

There are a few general issues that can help distinguish between healthy and unhealthy sexual behavior. The first of these is the theme of respect that must be reflected in all behavior. The second is the element of boundaries that are personal to the individual and to others. Finally, sexual behavior is a form of communication and the question is what a particular behavior is communicating—a healthy positive message or a negative unhealthy one.

Respect is fundamental to healthy sexual behavior--respect for self and for others. Some children disrespect their own bodies by self-harm or intentionally causing pain. Such behavior can be an indication of prior sexual abuse that can cause self-loathing and inflicting pain because the child believes this is what they deserve. When sexual behavior reflects a theme of self-harm, pain or injury, it is time to seek some professional help. Respect for others is also important for sexual behavior to be healthy. There are many problematic behaviors that do not take into account the well-being of the other person, and in this way they do not show respect for the best interest of others. Problem behaviors can include exposing genitalia with the intent to shock or gain negative attention. The age of the child as well as the motivation and the circumstance are important here. A young child who would rather not wear clothing is different than a young teen who exposes himself to another child because he knows it is wrong and will get a reaction. Other problem behaviors include touching others in games or activities with the intent to be sexual. Seldom do children consider the other person when they demonstrate intentional sexual touching in play because the other child is there to play the game, not to be involved in something sexual. Many young people make prank phone calls, but saying something sexual with the intent to shock fundamentally lacks respect and consideration for the other person.

Boundaries are always important in relationships. Sexual boundaries are some of the most important that we teach children. Teaching children safe and healthy sexuality must include attention to boundaries, our own and others. Boundaries are often directly connected to beliefs and cultural norms. Certain statements, clothing and actions may be accepted in one culture and strongly prohibited in another. The important point about boundaries is that we need to be direct and clear with children just where boundaries are drawn when it comes to sexuality. If we leave this issue up to the child to learn from daily experience, we must remember that our society is presenting in the media, entertainment, music and video games, modeling that is often very different than the boundaries you want your child to learn. In the absence of you teaching the child, the unhealthy sexual boundaries will be what the child learns.

Since sex involves communication, the question must be asked what is being communicated? Some of the unhealthy messages that sexual behavior can communicate include: I want to use you for my own gratification, I will try to get you to do something you don't want to do, or my interests are more important than yours. What sexual behavior communicates is another example that it is less what the behavior is than the who, what and why surrounding the behavior. Few sexual behaviors always have the same meaning and communicate the same message. Like all behavior, to understand sexual incidents it is important to look at what is being communicated by the child – is it naïve curiosity and experimentation or is it trickery and taking advantage of someone who is vulnerable?

Sexual Behaviors that Are of Concern

All children are capable of both healthy and unhealthy sexual behavior. Many behaviors may be unwanted or inappropriate but need nothing more than vigilance and a higher level of supervision to prevent. However, there are others that should be given extra consideration because they could indicate a need for professional help. Here are behaviors that Dr. Cavanagh Johnson lists as concerning (2013).

Preoccupation with sex – although children show an interest in sex, normally they do not maintain the interest and they move on to something else that is more interesting at the moment. When children seem to have a fixation on sexuality, it can be a sign that something is wrong and more attention is warranted.

Sex play with much younger children – it is very unusual for very young children to engage in sex play unless they have been exposed to such behavior by an older person. If a very young child is exposed to sexual behavior, this is of concern.

Precocious knowledge beyond the child's age – in the same way sex play does not occur to very young children, it is important to monitor if a child is demonstrating a knowledge and/or interest in sex beyond their age. This may be another sign of concerning exposure to sex from someone older.

Unusual sexual interests – an unusual sexual interest may be causing pain to self or another, themes of control and dominance, or repetitive behavior that may be a sign that the child has had a sexual experience leading to being preoccupied with sex.

Drive to act out sexually – children are spontaneous and are driven to be active, explore, engage in novel activities and other pursuits that could be generally considered play. However, if a child appears driven to sexual activity over other play, this may be of concern.

Sexual Exposure

The first issue people think of with very early exposure of a child to sexuality is sexual abuse. With the prevalence of sexual abuse this possibility must be considered. However, there are many other potential sources of sexual themes such as cable TV, magazines and movies, and the amount of pornography in our culture is unfortunately bound to find its way into the hands of children. Although any of this exposure could be concerning, just because children show consistent interest in sex or seem knowledgeable of sex beyond their age, it may not be an indication of sexual victimization by an adult or older child.

Sex play has a negative impact on other children – healthy sexual activity with children should have the themes of other childhood play. Any play activities that disadvantage an involved child should be of concern to supervising adults. The same is true for any sex play.

51

Seeing others as sex objects – children with healthy connections are very personable and drawn to people. Any theme of treating people as objects, whether in the sexual realm or in everyday communication, is an issue of concern.

Violate rights and boundaries of others – it is not unusual for children to have a poorly developed personal space or to intrude on the boundaries of others. However, if this is true of sexual behavior it is of concern because sexual privacy and boundaries are an essential area they must learn as young as possible.

Was the question for shock value?

A member of our Board of Directors who was a priest came for dinner one night right after the sex education group. One young child inquired at dinner, "Father are you proud of your penis?" The priest stammered and said he had not really thought about it before, but he replied, "Well I suppose I am." After dinner he learned the group ended just before dinner. Was the child crossing a boundary? There is no question that what is discussed in a sex education group may not be the best topic at dinner with company. But in this case, the young man wanted to show the priest that he was learning from the program and it was not meant to shock anyone. This is an example that the meaning and context of the behavior is as important as the behavior itself.

Should not experience fear, shame, and guilt – if the sexual behavior of children is healthy, there may be a tone of being covert due to doing something they know they should not be doing, but emotions of shame and guilt reflect a more serious tone and may be a sign of prior concerning sexual contact.

Adult-like sexual activity – children have sexual interests in many areas, they are interested in what is under clothing, in differences in bodies and touching body parts. However, if sexual behavior mimics adult-like sexual behavior, then a possible concern is whether the child has had or witnessed sexual contact with an adult or older child.

Directing sexual behavior toward adults – anytime a child is viewing an adult as a focus of sexual attention, this brings up a concern for past experience with an adult.

Sexual activity with animals – sexually touching an animal is not unusual for some children, but it is reflecting either a lack of understanding an important boundary or it reflects a concerning interest in sexual contact with a pet or farm animal.

The use of sex to hurt others – any theme of causing pain, getting back at someone or showing a serious lack of consideration for another person is concerning from both a sexual perspective as well as a serious lack of empathy.

Bribery, threats, force to engage other children in sex play – the theme of coercion related to sexual behavior should always raise concerns. The more sophisticated the coercion is, the more concerning it should be because it reflects an understanding that a behavior is unwanted and the child's behavior is an attempt to ignore the issue of consent and violate the space of another person.

The Ten Commandments of Healthy Sexual Behavior

One mistake many adults make is thinking that healthy sexuality is about biology and knowing body parts and functions. Very little of the complex topic of sexual health is what is covered in science class, it has much more to do with psychology class. Jan Hindman addresses healthy and unhealthy sexual behavior in her book There Is No Sex Fairy

(2006). One way she addresses the issue is in her "Ten Commandments of Healthy Sexual Behavior." The importance of these ten factors makes it worthwhile to say a little about each one.

1. Start young to teach biology as well as respect. Many adults become uncomfortable teaching about sex, in part, because they wait too long. When instruction begins at young ages, most adults feel more prepared to give general information and children are often more open to this topic at younger ages. Discomfort can enter the picture when parents believe they need to give greater detail and often assume (sometimes correctly) that the young person already knows a considerable amount, but often not helpful or even correct sexual information. When an adult starts sharing sexual information at a young age, they can build on information as the child matures. All parents will be more comfortable talking about the key area of respect than the details of where babies come from. And this is a major point of this book, one of the most important aspects of sexual health comes down to respect. Respect for ourselves, our body, respect for other people and the boundaries and feelings of others. Without respect entering the realm of biology, body parts and functions, there cannot be sexual health.

2. Communicate -- Children are learning from many sources, they need to learn from you. Several sources of sexual information have already been mentioned. As they are listed, make a mental note of which ones you want to rely on to provide your child with an understanding of sexual health: movies, magazines, television, video games, music, advertisements, peers, the internet, and newspapers. Are any on your list? What children need is sufficient context to be able to understand that a brand of cologne will probably not attract the person you are interested in like the ads show, but being yourself you have a much better chance to make the person a friend. How can a child be prepared to go through life and not be seduced by empty promises and come-ons that often use sex as the bait? You must provide children with the ability to respect themselves when others might not. How does a child learn that a sexually healthy person is neither phobic nor fixated on sex? Health requires integrating their maleness or femaleness in all they do and models respectful touch, affection, boundaries and intimacy. Don't wait for the 'sex talk' to integrate sexual information into daily life where it belongs. This will help prevent sexual information from being hidden and relegated to secret internet searches or the magazine under the mattress. It is healthy to discuss and learn about sex, have your child learn important information from you and learn it is OK to want to know more about sex; we all do.

You can ask me anything about sex.

Have you ever found yourself saying this to a child, "you can ask me anything"? In one of my classes after opening the question period with this statement, one of the crafty children asked, "OK, what sexual positions do you use with your wife?" In a matter of fact way I said boundaries around sex are important, and I was going to show that by saying the question asked for my own private information and we all need to learn the boundary of what is private. I learned that day to not start with "you can ask me about anything."

---

3. Teach logic -- rules, robbery, and rescue. Many adults wonder how to approach the delicate topic of sexual abuse, sex crimes and topics such as rape. I like how Jan Hindman frames this topic under rules, breaking the rules and what to do when rules are broken or what she describes as rules, robbery and rescue. We don't get purple faces when we talk about a bicycle being stolen. All children know taking something that is not yours is against the rules and it is wrong. When someone breaks the rules of your private space or boundaries, in a real way they are robbing you of what is rightfully yours. It may not be your backpack or your bicycle, but you have been robbed just the same when someone breaks sexual rules with you. If this happens, just like any robbery, get help. Young people need not be ashamed to report any robbery, and when they do adults need to be ready to step-up and come to the rescue with understanding, compassion and a willingness to help out. Unless these areas are clear to a child, there will be a natural reluctance to report a problem related to sex. Speaking out when something private of theirs has been tampered with is important. Children must believe there is rescue available even if the bad person is a member of the family or a friend of the family, which is the case with over 90% of sexual abuse.

4. Don't keep children from the world--teach children healthy information and critical thinking. Here lies another dilemma for adults, should I be honest about the bad things that go on in the world and risk scaring the child? Some families decide that they want to keep the child from knowing the worst aspects of the world for as long as possible. The question must be asked who are these adults protecting? Children know there is a lot of bad in the world, they know that things break, pets die, people say and do hurtful things, bad things happen, and there are jails for bad people who do bad things. In most fairy tales, there is evil as well as good and I still have a visceral response to remembering the first time *Bambi* was read to me. If you want to truly prepare and protect children, let them know that danger does not only come from speeding cars in the street, but also from someone trying to violate your personal space or your privacy. Children must learn to question right from wrong, who to trust and who not to, and these questions lead to higher order mental reasoning that can come in handy in a host of situations in the future as they travel into a world that is full of both good and bad.

To be helpful you must be understood.

When I was in elementary school my very serious Grandmother, in a moment of distress, took me aside and told me to be careful of strange men who hung around public toilets and bothered themselves. I can only guess that she read in the paper that someone was arrested for masturbating in public. But my young mind had insufficient information to understand this warning. I wondered why someone would bother himself in the first place and why it was any concern of mine. In her attempt to help me, Granny confused the issue by not being sure I understood her point.

---

5. Teach gender equality and the meaning of consent. Males and females are not the same but they are equals and deserve equal respect. Here is another place where a parent cannot rely on the culture to teach sexual equality when our culture still does not treat females as they treat males (such as females making 77% of wages males make for the same work). You must teach gender equality and do so by example in everyday life. A child must see equality demonstrated in what happens in the home. Equality is directly connected to consent. It is no more the job of a female to please a male than the reverse. Women and children must no longer be viewed as property, as in times past, and therefore they have a voice in who, when and how they interact with others. Consent is all about reciprocity and a two-way street. Both individuals must agree, whether it is what game to play or what form of touch is wanted. Consent is active agreement not only with words but also with energy; less than this is not true consent.

6. Sexual respect goes beyond biology and nature. Respect is not automatically learned. The dictionary says that respect is to acknowledge the good, the value, and the importance of something or someone (Merriam-Webster, 2014). If information about sex stops with biology, such as body parts and functions and does not include the good, the valuable and the important role sex plays in our lives, than our instruction is insufficient. If the value and goodness of sex is not a part of the curriculum, than sex is merely facts and mechanics and therefore why consider it anything more than a vehicle for gratification? Sexual respect will seldom be found in movies, magazines and locker room talk; it must be learned, and if not from you then from whom?

7. People don't end up bad if bad things are done to them. Teach resiliency and personal responsibility. It is an unfortunate reality that far too many children are initiated into sexuality by being abused. In fact millions of young people have their first sexual experience through the frightening event of being tricked, manipulated or forced into behavior they did not or could not consent to. The data points to 20% to 25% of males and females being sexually victimized before adulthood. That could be 15 million children! The children who have had the experience of being used by another for sexual gratification have been taught the worst lesson about sex – that respect and consent are not involved. They may grow up and pass on this terrible attitude. Others may end up emotionally damaged and associate their very worst experiences with sex. All children need to learn that if someone hurts you, the responsibility is theirs and not yours, and you are not bad if someone treats you badly. Teaching resiliency or the ability to bounce back after adversity is one of the most important lessons a child can learn, whether it is falling off a bike or having someone violate your private sexual space.

8. Teach delaying gratification and self-esteem. In a famous study at Stanford University with a name (the Marshmallow Study) not consistent with its importance, the ability of young children to delay gratification and not eat a marshmallow for 15 minutes predicted a significant difference in success in later life (Mischel, Ebbeson & Zeiss, 1972). Children who learn to delay for later what they may want immediately have an ability they can use throughout their life in education, economics, relationship and sexuality. One of the many differences in the Stanford study between the child who could and those who could not delay what they desired was a higher level of self-determination, an important component of self-esteem. Sexuality is an important area to learn delaying gratification where the appetites of the body must be controlled not by our brain's desire system (nucleus accumbens), but by our higher reasoning center (pre-frontal cortex). We must teach our children a thoughtful middle ground between 'if it feels good do it' and 'if it feels good it must be bad so avoid it.' We must teach our children that you must be in thoughtful control of yourself to be a strong person with a strong sense of self value (self-esteem). Delaying gratification can be helpful far beyond sexual choices as the Marshmallow Study reflects. Give your child the many advantages of learning control over desires early in life.

9. Teach RESPECT -- vulnerability of others, healthy guilt, restitution, feelings of others, anti-bullying. There are several important topics in Commandment 9. Perhaps the most important is to act contrary to one's animal instincts and do not take advantage of vulnerability. In nature it is the slow, the weak and the young that become the easy prey for the predator. Human aspirations rise above this tendency and protect rather than prey upon vulnerability. For the many children who have been on the receiving end of sexual victimization, learning to protect the vulnerable is even more essential. Guilt is often referenced as an unnecessary and even neurotic feeling, but guilt is directly connected to a person's conscience and sense of right and wrong. Physical pain plays a role to know what to avoid to protect our body. Healthy guilt plays a role to avoid violating our code of moral behavior. Restitution should be taught to children early – if you harm someone or something, you make it right. If someone steps over the line of someone else's emotional or physical boundaries, it is important to take responsibility, express true regret and make amends. A sexually healthy person must understand empathy or connecting with the feelings of others. If you teach each of these important moral principles, than you likely don't have to talk about each of these areas from the negative perspective of avoiding bullying behavior.

10. Teach touching and tenderness with modeling at all ages. Touch is a form of communication, in fact it is the first language we learn. Touch is a basic need and in the long run no less important than other basic needs. But touch can communicate many messages from helpful to hurtful. Teach your child the importance of supportive touch that communicates caring and love and do so at all ages. Young people do not lose their basic need for touch, despite their attempts to convince you that they are "all grown up now." If they were grown up they would have insight that teen years are some of the most difficult periods of life and the need for touch actually increases just when the young person may stop initiating physical closeness from you and other supportive adults. Don't wait for an invitation, meet your own need for touch by frequently initiating caring touching of all kinds with your children at all ages.

Making up for lost touch.

My father spent 22 years as an officer in the United States Air Force. When I was young he seemed most comfortable, at times, attempting to interact with his children the same way he did airmen in the military. Some of his early parenting was a bit stiff (remember side one of the sex record). Touch was put into categories, and as we grew up touch was much less available as we looked more like young airmen. However, when I was eighteen and left home he said to me that since I was a man we could now be friends, something I wish was available before I left home. My years of higher education taught me the importance of touch and although uncomfortable at first, I always initiated a hug rather than a hand shake with my father. He learned to love it and he started doing the same not only with me but with my brothers and his friends and family. I remember having to prepare my future wife for visits to my parent's home because I told her that my father was touch deprived by his own doing for many years, and now he was catching up on what he missed.

The CERTS Model

Champions can be found in the area of healthy sexuality. Jan Hindman has been mentioned as one such champion on the issue of sex and another person who has formed her professional career around healthy sexuality is Wendy Maltz, L.C.S.W. who developed the CERTS Model of healthy sexuality. The CERTS Model, not surprisingly, aligns well in many of the same issues in Hindman's Ten Commandments of Healthy Sexual Behavior discussed previously. CERTS stands for:

Consent – this is a simple and yet complex concept since it is not merely resisting or going along with something initiated by another person. True consent is to freely choose to take part in something that the individual is mature enough to know what they are agreeing with and its possible consequences. By this definition consent is never present between a child and someone much older. Consent also requires that the individual has a true choice and could decline at any time.

Equality – it is an important gender component and also an interpersonal element. It is important to see others as fundamentally equal as individuals, and with another person the level of personal power and dominance is close enough to equality for there to be no element of coercion or intimidation.

Respect – this is fundamental to healthy sexuality to have a belief and value that you give to yourself and to others. Respect must be operationalized between people and this is particularly important in interactions with another person that are sexual.

Trust – this requires that you allow yourself to be vulnerable in interactions with another person and believe that you will not be intentionally harmed either physically or emotionally in the process. Trust requires a level of compassion and sensitivity to the needs of others and to expect the same in return.

Safety – this is a fundamental need and right of an individual, and particularly in interactions with others. "It has to do with taking steps to ensure one's own and one's partner's physical and emotional well-being. Safety allows sexual experiences to be free of anxiety and fear. Partners are committed to preventing negative outcomes such as unwanted pregnancy, injury, insult, and disease. Safety in sexual experiences creates a level of comfort and naturalness free of worry, guilt or distress—establishing opportunities for increased sexual pleasure" (Maltz, 2014).

Maltz and Hindman include nearly identical concepts when they operationalize healthy sexuality, and it lends credence that both see the importance of respect, consent, safety and each of the other components. Both help demonstrate that promoting healthy sexuality is so much more than talking about body parts and biology.

Developmental Impacts of Sexual Abuse

Many children have had sexual trauma of one type or another, and many of these children live with this fact in silence without most adults in their life knowing this is the case. Because of this, a review of the negative impacts of sexual trauma deserves some attention. With children who have experienced sexual trauma, the job of an adult to help the child achieve sexual health is made significantly more difficult. All children respond somewhat differently to abusive experiences because trauma is not what happens to the child but what the child internally experiences. The same experience can result in very different responses due to age, background, and the support the child receives. The following are the consequences that most often take place following sexual trauma.

Having sexual contact long before having the emotional capacity to cope – there are many potentially positive aspects to sexual contact, including closeness, pleasure and feeling wanted and important to someone; however, sexual victimization robs the experience of all positive aspects. Sexual intimacy with someone who is older, larger or more dominant is almost always confusing, if not frightening and traumatic to a child. The limited times sexual abuse is not frightening or bewildering, the child is faced with physical contact that they are too young to put into any perspective and coping in a positive way with such an experience is extremely rare.

What is a traumatic experience?

Trauma has more to do with an internal experience than what happens to a person. When the brain defines an experience as threatening or frightening, it goes into survival mode and attempts to react through the fight or flight response. If the brain senses it cannot eliminate the threat, the experience can be perceived as life threatening and can cause a traumatic response regardless of the external event. So some children are sexually abused by someone known to them (most sexual abuse fits this pattern) and they do not experience threat and trauma, while other children experience the significant psychological damage of trauma. To know if the child has been traumatized requires consideration of not just what has happened but how the child perceived the event.

Most of the impacts of sexual trauma have been known for decades, such as the following list from research in 1985 (Finkelhor & Browne, 1985).

Sexual interests start very young – it is not just physical changes that start early, but attention and fixation on sexual themes are much more pronounced with many children who have had sexual trauma. It is as if the sexual light switch has been turned on by the early sexual experience and it is very difficult to turn the switch off.

Increased likelihood of sexually reactive behavior – increased sexual interests often leads to increased sexual behavior. This is often termed sexually reactive behavior as opposed to sexually offending behavior.

Increased likelihood of further sexual abuse – sexual abuse is associated with a list of subsequent predictive experiences including: internal conflicts, relationship troubles throughout life, mental health issues, substance abuse and further sexual victimization. As you would expect, sexual abuse does not predict any positive outcomes.

Depression – there are both psychological and chemical components of depression. Sexual abuse is correlated with both components as the individual matures and enters both teen and adult years.

Self-destructiveness – higher incidents of self–harm have been found to be present among the victims of sexual assault. This can be one outgrowth of feeling used, treated like you have little value and the seemly illogical fact that the victim begins to victimize him or herself after being traumatized by someone else.

Anxiety attacks – mood issues such as intense stress and anxiety are directly associated with traumatic experiences that are sexual in nature.

Nightmares/sleep problems – there are many theories on the role of sleep and dreaming and one is that dreaming both relives waking experiences and attempts to resolve internal conflicts. Both of these themes fit with the fact that nightmares and sleep disorders are common after sexual trauma.

Somatic complaints – physical problems that do not have a physical cause are not just associated with young abuse victims. Many adults who were sexually traumatized as children develop a variety of somatic disorders, and the medical community is considering whether the volume is turned up on the pain receptors following trauma.

Eating disorders – this very familiar outgrowth of sexual trauma could have several associations. Some victims want to become safe believing they can become unattractive and unapproachable by over-eating. Other individuals can develop anorexia nervosa or bulimia, which are associated with internal conflicts. All eating disorders can be categorized as internalizing disorders where the individual causes self-harm by internalizing their distress.

Dissociation – a classic outgrowth of abuse involves the psychic numbing or becoming unresponsive to external stimuli consistent with dissociating from awareness of the present environment. This condition is more frequently experienced by females than males and by more young children than older children. Generally the more helpless the individual perceives their situation, the more likely they are to dissociate.

Low self-esteem – another outgrowth of sexual trauma is the nearly universal experience of a lack of self-worth. People who are victimized often wonder what they did to cause the abuse and believe there must be something about them that would have someone treat them with so little respect. When the victim turns responsibility inward, the result can be some level of loss of self-respect.

Interpersonal relationship problems – all sexual abuse is caused by another person and therefore there must be a relational aspect to the trauma. When someone is victimized, the brain responds often with self-protective adaptations such as becoming distant, avoiding closeness and being unwilling to trust and be vulnerable to another person. All relationships require levels of trust and vulnerability and, therefore, relationships are negatively impacted by trauma.

Isolation – the world of victimization is almost always a solitary world. Children are abused in secret and it is usually made very clear to the child that no one is to find out. This secretive theme begins the path to loneliness and suffering in isolation. After the abuse, the individual thinks that no one will believe the truth, and since something obviously bad has happened and they were involved, then they deserve to be punished. Although this may not be logical, it is common among children after sexual abuse.

Puberty starts sooner – studies have shown that menses in girls and elements of puberty in boys begin earlier following sexual trauma (Mendle, Leve, Ryzin & Natsuaki, 2013).

Additional impacts of sexual trauma have been added over time to the growing list, including the following (Kendall, Williams & Finkelhor, 1993):

Betrayal of trust produces a mistrustful internal working model – John Bowlby who developed attachment theory coined the term internal working model as a description for how an individual perceives things. When you are abused it is a violation of trust and trusting anyone after such an experience is difficult and goes against the brain's primary focus of self-protection.

Hypersensitivity to sexual themes – trauma produces an excessive focus on a number of themes such as safety, protection and control. Another theme is linking sex to common situations with the child reactive, anxious and also fascinated by sex. Sex becomes front and center to the child's awareness and this theme comes out in many forms, most of them inappropriate and negative.

Avoidance of adults who want something – after an adult uses a child for sexual gratification, the child's brain adapts to being sensitive to anyone else who wants something, then the child avoids the person. The brain does not discriminate and the child avoids teachers who want something from the child, parents and any adult the child senses wants something, even though it may be positive.

Sexualizing motivation and behavior of others – the hypersensitivity to sex can produce in the child the perception that sex is a factor in the motivation of other adults and children. Since the child's brain does not know for sure, it assumes the worst to insure protection. This dynamic makes it difficult for the child to get beyond their trauma when they see threats in every direction.

Loss of correctly understanding the interests and messages of others – similar to assuming sexual motivations, sexually abused children incorrectly read sexual themes into the communication of others. Not only does the child react once again to a potential threat, but also misses whatever the actual message was.

Excessive self-protection – when the child's brain perceives constant sexual themes and threats that are not real, a great deal of energy goes into self-protection. This over-activation of protective responses causes the child to miss a great deal going on in the environment, which is one reason why sexual trauma can produce learning difficulties in school and other places.

Avoidance of intimacy and vulnerability – this is perhaps the easiest of all the negative impacts to understand. Why would a child have any interest in being close and vulnerable after having the experience of being used and abused by someone with more power?

Fear of the internal drive to join with a love interest – the drive to attach to others at all stages of life is instinctual. However, for children who have experienced sexual trauma this instinctual drive produces fear in the child and the result is the opposite of what the instinct is attempting to facilitate, which is comfort and support. Untreated sexual abuse can extend this theme to adults who avoid developing close loving relationships as adults.

After such a formidable list of negative side effects of sexual trauma, it should be abundantly clear how much more difficult it is to promote healthy sexuality for individuals who have had the worst possible initiation into sex.

Is sexual health possible after sexual trauma?

There is nothing easy about it, but individuals who have had sexual trauma need not be victims and they need not carry with them unresolved anger and pain caused by sexual abuse. There is help available and there are some very good resources to help with the journey (Ziegler, 2009; Maltz, 2001; Davis, 1990). The sooner the road to sexual health is started, the better the chance to reach it.

Sexual Behavior from Sexually Abused Children Can Still Be Healthy

Although some would disagree, just because a child has been exposed to sexual abuse should not mean that all sexual behavior after such an experience by definition would be of concern. It only makes sense to take the opposite stance that by definition since children are sexual beings, that despite their experiences there is a possibility that some behaviors are normative and healthy. This point is being made due to the pattern by many to call all sexual behavior after sexual abuse "sexually reactive" behavior. Certainly much of the result of sexual abuse is sexually reactive behavior, but not necessarily all behavior. Since so many children are exposed to sexual abuse of one type or the other, to say that none of these children can have healthy behavior afterward is unfair and inaccurate. It is important for adults who are faced with sexual issues with children who have experienced abuse to avoid overreacting and seeing pathology when it is not there. Not only do children who have been sexually abused need to be understood and helped to put sex into proper perspective, these children need understanding more than children who have not been abused. Seeing some type of disturbance any time an abused children reflects that they are sexual beings is not the type of understanding the child needs. Therefore, it is important to be able to tell healthy, normal behavior from the unhealthy, concerning behavior.

The Challenge with Sexually Abused Children

The objective of this part of the book has been to help clarify what is and is not healthy. The first step for an adult is to not become reactive to sexual issues and to think through the situation because there is no substitute for clear reasoning. However, when it comes to helping children who have had sexual trauma, there are many more challenges in promoting healthy sexuality than for children with no past abuse. We will end the discussion with some suggestions on the more challenging population of children with sexual trauma.

Perhaps the greatest challenge in helping a child who has experienced sexual trauma is to gain the necessary trust so the child is not using self-protective strategies that interfere with learning. It is not hard to see why some level of trust is essential — the child must be open to the presence of the adult rather than to avoid, to listening rather than ignore, and to believing the adult's motivation is to help rather than hurt. There are at least two essential requirements of gaining trust with children who have experienced trauma – consistency and time. The fundamental challenge is to communicate to the child's brain that survival mechanisms can be turned off (the amygdala sounding the alarm and the hippocampus initiating the stress response cycle resulting in fight or flight behavior). The only means to connect with the child's brain is to avoid any similarities to past experiences and to convince the brain that you are not a threat. This can be done by insuring that the child's basic needs are met regardless of the child's behavior. It is essential to make sure that the child does not experience any threat to receiving his or her basic needs, and this takes some extra care.

Incentives for traumatized children must be carefully considered. For example, it is not recommended to use food incentives as either rewards or corrective consequences. The reason for this is when an adult provides food (a basic need) for good behavior or restricts food (missing dessert) for poor behavior, the child's brain sees that at any time food could be withheld. It is important to remember that touch is a basic need and once again the child's brain cannot experience that touch may be withheld for poor behavior, such as

71

inappropriate sexual behavior. Love is a basic need and when a child makes a mistake or breaks a family rule, the child's brain will be looking for reassurances that love has not been lost. Therefore, do not physically distance yourself from a child after he or she has done something wrong or it will send the wrong message. The traumatized child's brain is hypersensitive to basic needs and it looks for consistent patterns. Therefore, even periodic failure to provide basic needs raises doubts in the child's brain and it continues to react with self-protection. Consistency is essential.

The second requirement is time. Many children have learned that abusive adults may 'groom' a child to let down their guard and then sexually harm them. Because of this, consistent responsiveness to the child over time is required. Safety and trust are not easily gained after sexual trauma. Once again, the issue of consequences for poor behavior is important. The child is not convinced by receiving basic needs for good behavior, it is when the child seriously breaks the rules that the child's brain will be particularly sensitive to any restriction of basic needs. It can take six or more months of being consistently non-threatening before the traumatized child begins to reduce self-protective reactivity—the first required step to forming trust. The time it takes to form even a basic level of trust is one reason that therapeutic approaches like brief therapies and short-term therapies are not effective or recommended for traumatized children.

Traumatized children avoid vulnerability at all costs. They have experienced being used and abused due to the vulnerability of being smaller and less in control than adults. However, the process of teaching something to a child requires a level of vulnerability for the child to be open to learning. The only cure for this problem is for the child to learn over many experiences that the past will not be repeated and vulnerability will not result in abuse.

A further complication following trauma is the need to heal as a first priority. Trauma signals the brain to focus primarily on survival, not learning something new. Following sexual trauma, the child must heal from the experience first. This dynamic is one reason why many traumatized children have learning difficulties in school. The process of healing is complex and will not be covered in detail here, but healing is a different process than learning about sexual health (Ziegler, 2011; Ziegler, 2009). It is recommended that every child who has experienced sexual trauma should be evaluated by an experienced professional with the initial consideration given to receiving help to heal from that trauma.

How to Find the Right Help

The complexity of helping a traumatized child learn about healthy sexuality, including the difficult process of healing from the trauma, points to the question of what to do when the situation is more complicated than you are prepared to handle? This could include the following situations:

- You are not sure if what you are doing is helping or hurting
- You have difficulty understanding the meaning of a child's actions
- You are struggling not to react to the situation
- Or you are not sure what to do next

Then it may be time to seek professional help for ideas and for support. Finding the right professional is not always easy. One approach is to do an internet search in your area for psychologists/counselors who have advertised expertise in sexual issues or sex education. So place a call to three places:

your local mental health authority, which you can find in the phone book under government organizations. Next, call a local non-profit counseling organization and finally, a social service organization that does not offer mental health counseling, such as a Big Brother/Big Sister program. In each call briefly mention what you are looking for—"I am trying to find a professional to help me with my son regarding some sexual issues, could you please give me three resources." After you have talked to everyone see what names come up more than once in your conversations.

Next set up a meeting with yourself and the professional and explain what you are looking for. You must do your best in a short period of time to ask good questions to determine the experience, the expertise and the orientation of the professional. Most of all you must ask yourself, "do I believe this person can help me?" If the answer is no, don't go back, return to the list of referrals, and try again. With persistence you can find the help that will give you and your family considerably more peace of mind going forward.

The first two parts of this book have been building to Part III where the focus will be on practical methods to work with sexual issues with children.

Summary Points

➢ Normal is not the goal, just because behavior is normal does not mean it is necessarily healthy.

➢ Normal sexual behavior among children includes a broader range than most adults believe.

➢ Asking why children act in sexual ways results in very similar answers to why adults engage in sexual behavior.

➢ Healthy sex requires, at a minimum, the qualities of respect, boundaries, and communicating a message that is enhancing rather than demeaning.

➢ Healthy sexual behavior can still be inappropriate and not wanted in certain settings.

➢ Promoting healthy sexuality for children who have experienced sexual trauma adds multiple layers of difficulty. But it can be done and you are likely to learn more than the child.

➢ Promoting sexual health after sexual trauma becomes significantly more difficult and may require professional assistance and coaching.

Part III: Understanding and Responding In a Healthy Way to Unhealthy Sexual Behavior

You have come to the part of the book where we not only consider understanding what sexual behavior means and what causes it, but also what to do about it. When the subject of interventions for sexual behavior comes up what this almost always means is how to stop sexual behavior. I hope you can now see that to promote positive sexual health we cannot simply put a lid on a child's sexuality. But we also cannot have excessive sexual behavior, and there are times and places where no sexual behavior can or will be tolerated in children. Throughout this discussion I will continue to come back to the goal of developing healthy sexuality, not eliminating or hiding sexuality.

There is only one place to begin this discussion and that is with the only foolproof method to reduce or eliminate unwanted covert, sexual behavior from a child, and that is adult supervision. It would be ideal if this was one of many no-fail methods to reduce such behavior, but it is the only one I know. So if you are reading this and you have a situation in which you must do something immediately to prevent a child from sexually acting out, then consider all the ways you can increase supervision of the child to eliminate the risk.

I doubt if the above is what you wanted to hear, but it is the tough reality. Short of stopping unwanted sexual behavior by keeping ever vigilant direct supervision, there are other ways that will be covered in this part of the book to intervene with unhealthy behavior and promote healthy sexuality in children.

The First Focus for the Parent Must Be Inward

Just in case you went immediately to this section of the book, it is critical that you begin the task of promoting sexual health in a child with looking at yourself. This was covered in some detail in Part I, so if you skipped it then at some point go back and take the test and consider if you are a good role model of sexual health. This step is critical because children learn from who we are much more than what we say. Sex information cannot be restricted to 'the sex talk,' instead, what a child learns are the behaviors and attitudes they experience and observe from you at home. Here are a few do's and don'ts as we move into interventions:

What to avoid:

- Don't underreact or overreact to sexual themes coming from the child. Reactivity to sexual themes produces a number of outcomes, all of them bad. The general principle of learning theory and operant conditioning is that whatever gets attention gets repeated. Most sexual behavior by children is unwanted by parents, but overreacting is not the way to go. Overreacting also tells children that sex is different, special, taboo, secretive and children (as well as adults) are attracted to these qualities. Overreacting can signal to the child that you are upset and angry, and this can distance you from the child as well as tell the child that sex is inherently bad. Overreacting can also give the manipulative child a tool to use against you and gain negative power over your emotions and reactivity. Overreacting activates your primitive emotion centers of the brain and shuts down your higher reasoning centers. You are neither thoughtful nor creative when your primitive brain is engaged. So for a list of reasons, don't give sexual themes power and importance they should not have — therefore don't overreact.

On the other hand, don't underreact to sexual themes that need attention as were discussed in Part II. Just because you don't want to know about it or don't want to talk about it, does not mean sexual problems in children will go away or improve. There can be some life changing ramifications for some sexual behaviors that are not consistent with sexual health such as teen pregnancy, sexual victimization, criminal behavior, sexually transmitted diseases and HIV. Don't overreact but don't underreact to issues around sex.

- Don't confuse unwanted sexual behavior with immoral behavior. Morality is closely connected to sexuality, but this is tricky territory when helping a child develop sexual health. Moral reasoning takes place in a part of the brain that is one of the last areas to mature, and generally this area, the orbitofrontal cortex, is not fully developed until the early to mid-twenties. Long before this age, individuals will be interested in and will act in sexual ways. If the parent defines childhood behavior as morally bad, there is a good likelihood that the child will either learn that sex is bad or they believe that he or she is bad, both must be avoided. So what is a parent to do? The answer is to treat unwanted sexual behavior in young children the same as any unwanted behavior. It is not morally wrong to talk loudly, but a young child must learn not to do this at the movies. It is not morally bad for a young child to come out of the bathroom with his pants around his ankles, but this is not desirable behavior at church or at the mall. Teach a child the behavior you expect without the moral component until later in childhood when the moral context can be understood and not confused with either the self or sexuality in general.

- Don't teach a child to have the same unhealthy view of sex you may have learned. This assumes that you were raised like most other children where anything related to sex was avoided or forbidden. If this was not the case, then consider yourself quite fortunate. But if that was your upbringing regarding sexuality, then give your child or the young person you are helping a better start to a life where sex can be less anxiety producing, less guilt ridden and closer to the enhancing dimension of a person that it has the potential of being.

- Don't think curiosity about sex from young children is a sign of a disturbance. A child's job is to play and learn, and sex is like any other part of the world around children. They are curious, they want to learn more, and they want to experience. None of these tendencies are a sign of a sexual problem; rather they are a sign of natural and healthy development. But you will want to shape the child's behavior very early on with guidelines, expectations, and information that are consistent with a developing healthy orientation to sexuality.

- Don't try to figure out on your own how to raise a young person to have sexual health. Unless you have had excellent modeling in how to raise a sexually healthy child, don't try to do this without getting additional help, some of which is in this book. If the child you are working with has a background of sexual trauma, than it is even more important that you obtain consultation in how to handle the many challenges you will face.

What to do:

- ✓ Treat sexuality as you would any other topic – openly and directly. As Jan Hindman used to say, "Don't get a purple face when you work with children on sexual issues." Approach sexual themes with the same open and direct focus you would other topics you will face with a child – "Will I die some day?" "Why doesn't Jason want to be my friend?" "Is God real or just a story?" None of these issues are easy to explain but none would produce a purple face, neither should sexual issues.

- ✓ Teach a child when and where sexual behavior is acceptable rather than the 'just say no' approach. If talking about, learning about or being curious about sex is never acceptable, than when and how will sex become a positive aspect of the child's world? If a child wants to draw anatomically correct pictures than give some guidelines to do so at home but not at school. If a child wants to learn the physical differences between boys and girls then you teach them rather than a teenage cousin.

- ✓ Monitor your child's interests, attitudes and behaviors related to sex. Many adults don't want to know about what the child is thinking when it comes to sex. They mistakenly believe the longer the subject can be put off the better. This is not a good strategy because the child will be learning in the meantime and could be learning from all the wrong sources. As a parent be knowledgeable about where your child is in developing sexual thoughts and behaviors.

- ✓ Start early and bring up sexual issues often to develop a comfort level in the child, but mostly be comfortable with the topic yourself. It might be too late by the time you are reading this, but if not, start when the child is young so that sex can be a topic of discussion like the weather, nature and any other interesting topic.

✓ Use the opportunity to help a child in order to learn more about sexual health yourself. In a very real sense, even when we are helping someone else we are helping ourselves. When we teach something to someone, we are also learning. Helping a child develop healthy sexuality can be an excellent opportunity to become more sexually healthy yourself.

General Principles of Working with Sexual Behavior

Although every child and every situation is different, there are some general approaches to intervening with sexual behavior and sexual themes. Some of these have been briefly mentioned previously and some are new.

1. Remove the aura of sex and treat it as behavior. This theme has been mentioned previously, but it is easier said than done. Here are a couple suggestions:

➢ Don't give sexual behavior special attention or this will reinforce more problem behavior. A principle of behavioral reinforcement is that the more attention a behavior receives, the more likelihood it will be repeated.

➢ Approach unwanted sexual behavior as you would any problem behavior. Most adults do not have a problem correcting problem behaviors in children, so view sexual behavior as just another needed correction.

> ➤ When considering the causes of sexual behavior, first consider if the child wants attention before thinking it is pathology. Some examples will be provided later in this section that will include the issue of behavior designed to obtain attention. Children learn quickly what adults notice and sexual issues are at the top on this list.

2. Work on being more comfortable talking about sexual issues. Children can easily pick up your discomfort, which can cause either reluctance to pursue the issue further or create anxiety around sexuality.

> ➤ Children pick up what makes parents uncomfortable, if the child has an interest in gaining power, the parent's uneasiness gives the child the chance he or she is looking for to gain the wrong type of personal power.

> ➤ Rehearse situations in your mind as to what you might say or do. It is often a good idea to think of how you are going to start the conversation as well as the major points you want to get across to the child.

> ➤ Practice talking about a sexual issue with your spouse or a friend. The more you discuss any issue, the more you will be familiar with the topic and accustomed to discussing it.

3. See the child and not just the behavior. As distressing as the behavior may be, don't forget there is a child beneath the behavior, and your goal is to help guide the child to appropriate behavior.

> ➤ Address the problem behavior in a way that is unique to this child. Connect in ways that have been successful in the past with this child.

➢ Don't let the behavior either overwhelm you or distance you from the child, this may be what the child intended as a way to control you.

➢ Consider whether the behavior is meant to be a distraction so you do not see the frightened child underneath the protective layers. Like anger, sexual behavior can be a cover-up for a child's fears and lack of control over his or her life.

4. Translate the meaning of the behavior. All behavior has meaning and this topic will be considered in some detail in the next section.

➢ What is the meaning to the child? The meaning of behavior is often different to the child than to the adult; it is important to identify what the child is communicating in order to know how to effectively respond.

➢ What is the child saying through the behavior? Examples will follow to show how you can understand the child's behavior.

➢ Always consider whether the meaning relates to having power and control and/or getting negative attention. Start with the most probable translation which is often themes of attention and then power and control.

➢ Unless you know what the true problem is, you will not find a successful solution. The most common mistake adults make is to address the wrong problem or issue, and the result is generally a failed intervention.

5. Consult with a partner – we often need a reality check when dealing with sexual behavior. This step has the added benefit of making you more comfortable with the topic.

> ➢ Problem solve together; two heads are definitely better than one. Another adult may help defuse your emotional reactivity to the behavior.

> ➢ Make sure you are thinking clearly and responding effectively; sexual behaviors can be some of the toughest challenges for parents. Understand this is a difficult issue for most parents and don't be too critical of how you handle the challenge.

> ➢ Consult again after taking action to consider if the goal was achieved. At times it helps to get an outside opinion of whether there is progress, since you may be too close to the issue to see subtle improvement.

6. Don't minimize and don't catastrophize. Mistakes can be made in both directions, what is needed is a balanced response.

> ➢ Boys may be boys, but boys can also be perpetrators in some situations. Your child could be acting in concerning ways that should be looked into by a professional.

> ➢ The child may, in fact, be "going through a phase," but the phase may be serious. This is another reason to get a professional opinion that can help you feel more confident in how you are handling the situation.

> ➢ Don't make the problem more than it is. Consider the facts and what did and did not happen. Adults often make a sexual issue larger than it actually is.

> ➤ Problem sexual behavior seldom has the long-term implications many parents think it will. Do not allow yourself to project serious implications into the sexual behavior of children, such predictions are seldom accurate or helpful.

7. Expect children to be sexually curious. It is actually more of an issue if a child has little or no interest in sexuality. It is a part of every child's development and something we expect children to be naturally interested in.

> ➤ Sex is one of the most fascinating aspects of nature, children are naturally inquisitive. By not giving the topic either more or less attention than it deserves, the natural curiosity probably will not be exaggerated.

> ➤ Sexual experience usually heightens interest and this is also natural. The more energy the child has in the area of sexuality, the more adult supervision is recommended, particularly around other children.

> ➤ Despite the child's past, allow the child to have some natural and healthy interest in sex. Even if the child has an unfortunate history of sexual abuse, there must still be room for the child to be curious and have an interest in sexuality, and this can be natural and healthy.

> ➤ When providing sexual information, use a balance of offering enough for the level of the child, but not too much to create stimulation. Use your instincts as to how much information to share. You can also get some assistance from another adult or check on the internet for sites that discuss sexual information for children — but choose such sites carefully.

8. Be sure to replace every problematic behavior with an alternative appropriate behavior. Because all behavior has a purpose, it is important to replace a wanted behavior for every unwanted behavior.

> ➢ Provide appropriate touch in the place of problem touch. This is always a good strategy when a child has an issue with touch that you would like to eliminate. If the need for touch is met in other ways, the odds are better to reduce the problem touching.

> ➢ Teach boundaries when children invade the space of others. All children must learn to respect the boundaries of others. Start early and repeat often with this instruction.

Understanding the Meaning of Sexual Behavior

Many adults struggle to understand the meaning of a child's sexual behavior or they skip this step entirely. The challenge for the adult is to replace their own perspective and consider what is going on with the child. Although this sounds complicated, there are some suggestions that can help.

Step 1 – Put yourself in the position of the child.

Step 2 - Consider at least three possible translations of the behavior and to these three add two more — gaining attention and gaining control over you, your emotions and the situation.

Step 3 – From your knowledge of the child choose the most likely translation of the behavior and proceed as if you are correct.

All behavior has meaning, until you find the meaning you will not be able to intervene successfully. The above three steps sound a bit simplistic, so we will go further into how to successfully translate the message of the child's behavior.

Translating Is Essential to Understanding the Meaning of Behavior

One of the most important steps in working with sexual behavior in children is to take the time to understand what the behavior means, and only then can the best interventions be determined. If you think that all sexual behavior is the same than it is even more important that you consider what the child is communicating through the behavior. Both adults and children communicate various messages with different behaviors. The central point here is that until you understand the behavior, you will be trying to fix the wrong problem. For example, there can be a tendency to believe sexual behavior indicates a much more serious problem than may be the case. In order to find out if there is a serious issue, or if the child is frustrated and just wants the undivided attention of the adult, we need to do a bit of detective work and look for the meaning of the behavior.

A few examples may help to understand how to translate the behavior. Three case scenarios will be offered as well as the suggestions for handling the sexual behaviors.

Scenario One. Cheryl is a 7-year-old adopted Asian female with poor boundaries who has a bad habit of touching other children in their private areas when playing tag or standing in line at school. Cheryl is not a child with any known sexual trauma and lives in a nurturing home with responsive parents. The issues of poor boundaries have been observed since a short stay in preschool when other parents complained about her "touching problem," and her parents were asked to remove her. Now the issue of boundaries has become more pronounced in the public school setting with other children.

Translating Cheryl's behavior – the best information to translate her sexual behavior is from adults who know her well. The first step is to consider what Cheryl is saying through her behavior – what the problem is that is causing the symptom of getting into the space of others and touching them in ways that are against the rules. It is a good idea to come up with multiple possibilities because adults too often rush to a conclusion. Here are a number of possible translations in Cheryl's case:

- o   I simply like to touch others in their private areas.
- o   I want to be close to others and touching them is how I do it.
- o   I want others to feel uncomfortable by doing something they don't like.
- o   I let my hands connect with others because I don't know what to say.
- o   This is how I show my anger with others.
- o   I get noticed more when I get into the space of others.
- o   I don't get touched enough.
- o   I do whatever I want without thinking about it.
- o   I hear voices that tell me to touch people.
- o   I feel powerful when I force myself onto other people.

Without the advantage of knowing Cheryl, we must attempt to narrow down the possible translations because the choices represent very different messages from her. If you knew Cheryl you could go one by one and decide which possible translations are more likely than others. Since I know Cheryl, I will walk through them as an example of the process. Here is what the symbols mean in front of the message:

- This translation does not fit this child
+ This translation does fit and is a real possibility
++ This translation fits best for this child in this situation

○ - I like to touch others in their private areas. Although some of her touching could be considered sexual, this translation does not fit her.

○ ++ I want to be close to others and touching them is how I do it. This is a definite possibility and sounds like her.

○ - I want others to feel uncomfortable by doing something they don't like. She is not motivated to hurt others, so this does not fit her.

○ + I let my hands connect with others because I don't know what to say. Cheryl's social skills are underdeveloped and this translation is possible.

○ - This is how I show my anger with others. Cheryl is not a very angry child, but she touches others frequently. It is not just when she is angry, so this does not fit.

○ + I get noticed more when I get into the space of others. She definitely likes to be noticed, but it is more that she wants people to recognize her than to get negative attention like other children might.

○ ++ I don't get touched enough. The sheer frequency of the problem makes this a very real possibility. This does not mean she is neglected, it may just mean she desires more touch than she gets.

○ + I do whatever I want without thinking about it. No question she is impulsive, but it does not fit that she acts in a mean way toward others.

○ + I hear voices that tell me to touch people. Although this is the most unusual of the translations, she does not have hallucinations, but after consideration it could be true that Cheryl's brain directs her to make lots of contact with others (a mental voice within), and she needs to learn a better way to do this.

o   - I feel powerful when I force myself on other people. She is not an aggressive child, so this possible translation does not fit as well as others.

Knowing Cheryl, an adult (in this case me) goes through each possibility and considers if the translation fits her. ++ means it really fits, + means it is possible and – does not fit as well as other possibilities. It is often a good idea to have one or two 'long shot' translations to encourage the adult to not just stick to typical possibilities. In this case the item about hearing voices was added. The purpose of such possible translations is to think broader than a preconceived answer; thinking outside the box can help climb inside the child's world and outside of the adult's world for a moment. Looking at the above, we start with the items that fit best and there are two. Notice that the single pluses all are somewhat connected with the double pluses. So now we can put the most probable items together and we develop a hypothesis (which may be right or wrong) that Cheryl is saying through her poor boundaries and touching problem that she has a need and desire to touch and be touched more than currently, and she also likes to connect with other people and the closer the better. However, the touching problem itself stems both from her lack of impulse control and not knowing how to meet her needs in an acceptable way.

If you are saying this is guess work, you are absolutely correct, it is. However, it is an educated guess and nearly always the adult will understand what is going on before the child is able to do so. As long as adults do not overreact, get in a hurry and rush to conclusions, they actually do very well in determining the meaning of behavior.

We now have a possible translation for Cheryl's sexualized touching and boundary problems. The next step would be to consider how to address the problem, which we will do in the next section. But at this stage we are simply considering the best of the possible translations.

We may be wrong and we will consider how we know if we are wrong and what to do if we are, but for the moment let's say we are close to being correct. If so, than does Cheryl have a sexual problem? Not as much as she has a deficit of social skills. Is it a moral problem? No. Does she need professional help? Not really unless steps to correct the problem do not help.

The second scenario is a bit more concerning and complex, potentially more like the issues you are facing with your child. The child has had a much more difficult childhood than Cheryl and it shows in his behavior and motivations.

Scenario Two. Christopher is 11 and has lived in multiple foster homes after his parents lost their parental rights due to neglecting him. Recently the school called and asked his foster parent to attend a meeting to discuss a recent report that Christopher suggested to another boy that they sexually touch each other after school. It was not done secretly and several other boys heard the conversation. When confronted by the school principal, Christopher did not deny the behavior but had belligerent energy. It is not confirmed but it is suspected that due to poor parental supervision, he was exposed to sexual abuse in his early years. This suspicion is supported by Christopher's unusual interest in the subject of sex and he escalates quickly to being moody and negative if corrected or if the subject of his behavior comes up.

Translating Christopher's behavior – Christopher is a good example of the millions of children who have experienced abuse in their lives and go to public school each day. It is not always clear to the school what to expect of children like Christopher and detailed background information on children is often not available to school staff, if the information exists at all. In cases like Christopher's, the school is put in a difficult position. Even if the school staff understand that it is not abnormal or unusual for children to talk about sex, this particular behavior cannot be allowed for any number of reasons. So the issue is not whether to do something about the situation, it is to determine the best course of action. A good start could be to translate the meaning of the behavior.

Here are some possible translations of Christopher's behavior:

- o I am trying to say that I am gay.
- o I release some of my stress by sexual touch with another child.
- o I don't know how to make a friend and being sexual may work.
- o I was more interested in intimidating the other boy than sexually touching him.
- o I want to use sex to have power and control over others.
- o I want to get kicked out of school and this is a fast way to be successful.
- o I am trying to drive the other boys away and this will keep them distant.
- o I want to get negative attention and talking about sex always works.
- o I am so impulsive that I simply said what I was thinking at the moment.
- o I am being sexually abused in the neighborhood and I hope someone pays attention and comes to my rescue.

The above possibilities once again cover a wide range of translations and meanings. Most of the possibilities are familiar to those who work with either foster children or children who have experienced abuse. Some items have nearly opposite meanings. To narrow down the possibilities, the same process will be followed as Scenario One with an adult who best knows Christopher adding the translation symbols (-, +, or ++).

- o - I am trying to say that I am gay. This does not fit this child in either content or how he communicates what he wants others to know.
- o - I release some of my stress by sexual touch with another child. Although this is true for some children, it does not fit Christopher.
- o + I don't know how to make a friend and being sexual may work. He does poorly in reading the energy of others and his social skills are poor, so this is a possible translation.
- o ++ I was more interested in intimidating the other boy than sexually touching him. The boy Christopher chose to go to is not someone he normally likes and one of his usual problem behaviors is intimidation.
- o ++ I want to use sex to have power and control over others. This sounds a lot like Christopher and the control is likely more important than any sexual interest.
- o + I want to get kicked out of school and this is a fast way to be successful. With his frequent issues at school, an interest in being suspended would be possible.
- o + I am trying to drive the other boys away and this will keep them distant. Drawing negative energy to himself from peers and adults is a frequent issue, so this may be a factor — particularly since his statement was so public.
- o + I want to get negative attention and talking about sex always works. This could be correct but he would

> not need to necessarily focus sexual talk at another specific child.
>
> o - I am so impulsive that I simply said what I was thinking at the moment. This situation did not feel particularly impulsive as much as manipulative.
>
> o + I am being sexually abused in the neighborhood and I hope someone pays attention and comes to my rescue. Although this is not known, it is worth considering and looking into further. Obvious sexual behavior can be a cry for help.

After considering the most likely translations, we are left with two and they are similar— intimidating others and using any means to gain power and control. Both of these themes are often found in children who have been removed from their homes due to abuse or neglect. These children often cover up their fears with aggression and they compensate for feelings. These children often feel like they have no voice over what happens to them and they look for ways to feel some power and control, and sometimes this is directed to younger or more vulnerable peers. Once again, it is likely that Christopher does not have a sexual problem as much as he is using sex as the strongest behavior he can come up with to have some control and power in his life. We may be wrong, but until further information is received we will proceed with our educated guess.

Scenario Three. Johnathan is 6 years old and has very poor social skills. He has on two occasions tried to talk other children into sexual touching. Johnathan used to live in a blended family and is the only child of very young mother. She married a man with two children, but the marriage ended in divorce and he and his mother live in public housing. Johnathan's mother made some poor choices in the past with drugs, ending up with Johnathan being removed and in foster care while she was in drug treatment. The neglect of

Johnathan's early years have impacted him in a number of ways.

Translating Johnathan's behavior – he is very young and is a likeable child, yet he represents a risk to other children not only because he has attempted to initiate sexual touching but he has been quite persistent and without adults stepping in sexual incidents would have occurred. Johnathon's mother struggles to meet the requirements of her minimum wage job with long hours and seems to have little energy left over for Johnathon when he is home from school and day care. He is educationally-delayed and is still in preschool but is older and larger than the other children. The present question is whether he will be allowed to return to the preschool after the two near sexual incidents.

Here are some possible translations of Johnathon's behavior in trying to initiate sexual behavior with younger children:

- o Do you want to be my friend?
- o I do sexual things when I am anxious about not seeing my mom much.
- o I don't feel noticed unless I am aggressive with others.
- o I like to be around younger children because I am more like them.
- o I am a developing sex offender.
- o Sex is a way to have power over someone smaller than me.
- o My mom is sexually abusing me and I am signaling that I need help.
- o I like to have friends and be close to them but don't know how to best do this.
- o Sex play is fun and I used to do it with my step-siblings who are now gone.
- o Sexual touching feels good; I like to touch and be touched by others.

Looking over these possible translations there are two that are long shot translations, can you spot them? They are the fifth and seventh items. As stated previously, it is a good practice to stretch your thinking with such items. This helps to think broader than you may have otherwise and opens some new possibilities. The next step is to narrow down the items.

- o + Do you want to be my friend? Knowing Johnathon, his attempting to be sexual with other children seems more normative than pathological, so he may be reaching out in this way.
- o + I do sexual things when I am anxious about not seeing my mom much. This may be possible, there are other problem behaviors that may have a correlation with limited contact with Mom such as often being emotional, quick to tantrum and hitting himself.
- o - I don't feel noticed unless I am aggressive with others. He is not an aggressive child and this does not fit.
- o + I like to be around younger children because I am more like them. He has shown a greater interest in younger children likely due to his being emotionally and developmentally young.
- o - I am a developing sex offender. There is no good reason to think this is the case.
- o - Sex is a way to have power over someone smaller than me. Once again this does not fit this young man who does not show signs of hurting others.
- o + My mom or someone else is sexually abusing me and I am signaling that I need help. There are a number of red flags to possible sexual abuse, foster care and being away from Mom, poverty, a mother involved in drug use at one point. This is a possibility worth considering, although probably not the case.

o ++ I like to have friends and be close to them but don't know how to best do this. This fits Johnathon the best of any item so far. He genuinely likes other children and likes to play with them. He misses his former siblings and is with adults much of the day. At the same time, he is not sure how to make a friend.

o + Sex play is fun and I used to do it with my step-siblings who are now gone. We don't know if there was sexual activity in his previous family, but it is possible.

o ++ Sexual touching feels good, I like to touch and be touched by others. We must consider the reality that sex is not only fun for adults, it can be fun for children as well.

Reviewing the above possible translations, the educated guess is that Johnathon's invitations to sexual activity is likely in the category of normative sex play. It is not what the pre-school teachers or parents of the other students want to happen in the school, but it is likely not a sign of a serious disturbance. What best fits is that Johnathon at his young age and with his developmental delays wants to be friends and be close to other children younger than he is. At the same time, it is worth considering if he has been exposed to sexual touch from others, particularly older teens or adults because such exposure could change the meaning of the behavior. We will come back to these three scenarios when we discuss ways to intervene in sexual issues with children.

The Three Goals in Working with Childhood Sexual Behavior

Since sexual behavior can have many meanings to the child and can come in many forms and present anywhere on the continuum of healthy to a serious unhealthy concern, what is a parent to do when facing sexual issues? One way to answer this question is to consider some general goals that can be used with any child and any level of sexual behavior. The three goals with children and sexual behavior are to monitor, manage and maintain a positive message about sexuality. In order to do all of these you need to understand the meaning of the behavior as was discussed in the previous section on translating.

Monitor – it has been pointed out that a wise parent will not ignore or look the other way when it comes to sex but will consider what the young person knows, the level of sexual interest, and the amount and type of sexual behavior the child is exhibiting.   With this information the adult has the opportunity to make a positive impact on the child's sexual health.

Manage – this is what most parents primarily want to do with sexual behavior and that is to control it. Although this is very understandable, it is important that while managing behavior you do not communicate a negative message about sexuality. Much of the rest of this section of the book will be devoted to managing sexual behavior effectively.

Maintain – while it is necessary to put limits on sexual behavior, the ultimate goal of sexual health requires that the adult maintains and communicates a positive message about sexuality. This may be the most challenging of the three goals to achieve because it requires the adult to override understandable reactivity and take a long-range view. It is very difficult for a child's brain to understand a message that sex is bad now but it will become wonderful later. It is a much better message that some behaviors are good for adults, but not good for kids.

Suggestions in Responding to Sexual Behavior

We have addressed some goals in working with sexual behavior. We have also gone over some do's and don'ts. Before we take our three scenarios and consider some ways to intervene with problem sexual behavior, there are a few more general suggestions to consider. Some have been discussed, but they will be briefly repeated.

Overreacting produces all the wrong outcomes – more problem behavior, more focus on sex being bad and more interest in having control over the adult, to name a few. Children who are interested in having control over adults are specifically tuned into the emotional response of adults to the child's behavior. Of course not all children have control issues, but many who exhibit problem sexual behaviors have a need for control. The quickest way to give power and control to the child and to increase the amount of sexual behavior you would like to avoid is to emotionally react to problem behavior. Clearly, staying even—tempered in the face of sexual behavior is easier said than done. Nonetheless, it is a reality that what adults give energy to will be repeated more than what does not get a reaction. Without question behaviors must be corrected, but how this is done is very important. The best approach is to calmly get the child's attention without an audience of others observing, address the behaviors you want changed, and add two components to the correction. First, find some aspect of the child's behavior that you can compliment the child on in order to approximate what you want to see more of from the child. The second component is to let the child know that you believe the child is capable of doing better and point out a time when the child did, in fact, do better.

Effectively correcting behavior has several components

Don't let problem behavior continue or the child will get the message that you approve of what he or she has done. When and how you correct the child will add or subtract from your success. Be specific, point out in positive terms what you expect of the child. Find some aspect of what the child did that you can compliment and let the child know that you believe in the ability of the child to improve. For example, "Dustin, your teacher told me you have been drawing penises on your figures in art class. Males do have penises, but school is not the place to draw the private parts of people. Anytime you would like to draw pictures of people with penises, let me know and that would be fine if you do it at home. You are good at drawing people and I want you to learn where and when to draw what you are interested in." And importantly, do all of the above with a matter of fact tone and little emotional energy.

If you find it difficult to address sexual issues without frustration, embarrassment, anger or surprise, than this makes you a normal adult. However, the most effective adults will reduce future problem behaviors by staying cool and calm and not giving the child any control over their reactions. At times you may need to vent your emotions later without the child present. One thought that may help is to consider a problem sexual behavior as any other type of problem behavior, no more and no less important. Take the extra emphasis of sex out of the equation and address the behavior head on. For example, "Denise, I don't want you raising your dress and rubbing your private area when other people are around. If you have an itch, find a place to take care of it when you are alone. Let me know if you have a problem or need some help, like you are very good at doing." Don't assume that a sexual theme is always about sex, it may be about getting attention (few behaviors get as much negative attention from adults as sexual behaviors), gaining some power and control over the adult, reflecting poor social skills with peers, or it may be an itch rather than masturbation. Once again, finding out the meaning of the behavior from the child's perspective is important in determining if you are addressing the right issue.

In Part I there was a discussion of the influence of the environment on the sexual behavior of children. If you are finding yourself addressing more sexual themes than in the past, than it may be time to consider how much sexual stimulation a child may find in your environment. You may have to look around with a different set of eyes because what is not stimulating to you may not be the same for a child. In a home in our culture there are many potential sources of sexual stimulation. Magazines use sexual themes to sell perfume, clothing, jewelry and cars. Millions of homes have cable television with programing that includes sexuality. But you need not have cable TV because in any prime time evening any number of programs will include a direct or indirect sexual theme. The list does not stop here; news, books, advertisements in newspapers, music, fine art and a host of other sources of sexual stimulation may be impacting your child. The goal is not to have a sexually sterile environment, but rather to understand how a child is responding to themes of sexuality that are everywhere.

Scenario Interventions

To make suggestions on intervening with problem behaviors as practical as possible, three scenarios were provided above. The first steps were taken in each case to translate the meaning of the problem behaviors. In this section interventions will be discussed for these three examples. It is important to begin with the principle that no intervention will work with every child in every situation. In fact, it is critical to design a course of action for a particular child and for a specific situation.

Scenario #1 Interventions

Our first scenario was Cheryl, who represents the least disturbance in her behavior of the three. The translation that was identified was that Cheryl's problem behaviors were probably coming from her need and desire to touch and be touched and a desire to be physically close to others. Keep in mind that touch is a basic need and even though Cheryl is not neglected at home, we believe she is reflecting that she would like to touch and be touched more than she is at present. Like other basic needs, it is difficult to have too much of something like positive touch. For example, how does one have too much safety or too much air? We might all have the same basic needs, but how much of each will meet the desires of individuals will depend upon the person and the situation.

So given our working translation of Cheryl desiring more touch and physical closeness with others, we can now consider what we want to do to meet her need and perhaps reduce the problem behaviors of inappropriately touching others. It is recommended to initially consider a list of possible interventions and to narrow the list to a few. It is always a good idea to come up with a variety of possible steps to take because it is nearly always the case that adjustments will be needed if the first attempts to address the problem are not completely successful, and in some cases they may even increase the problem behaviors. If you have a list of possible interventions and your initial approach is unsuccessful, then you are ready to adjust your attention to the next intervention.

103

Here are a few of possible interventions to provide Cheryl more of what we think she is trying to obtain through her problem behaviors of touching others in sexual ways:

1. Increase the amount of touch Cheryl receives throughout the day. Often adults reduce the amount of touch they give children who demonstrate problem touching. You could make an argument that this makes some sense, however, this is often the opposite of what is needed.
2. Increase the amount of quality time Cheryl has with adults important to her. At times, touch is not the only need she has, she also wants to be the center of attention with important adults in her life.
3. Read Cheryl a story of a child who needed to learn how and when to touch others. If it is difficult to find the right story, it is suggested to make up a story that has the elements that fit a specific situation.
4. Increase the amount of positive attention Cheryl receives. Such a generalized intervention could help if some aspect of the problem behavior is the child not getting enough positive attention. It is common in these situations that the child begins to seek negative attention, which he or she may find easier to obtain.
5. Arrange adult mediated peer contact. The first principle of reducing unwanted sexual behavior is to increase adult supervision. While providing close supervision, put Cheryl in situations with peers but with an adult right there to prevent problem touching and demonstrate acceptable touch.

Many more possible interventions for Cheryl could be developed, but this short list offers the potential of reducing the problem behaviors. The adult who best knows the child can then identify two to three interventions to start with. Since I know Cheryl, the above interventions are rank ordered as follows: 1 – 4 – 2 – 3 – 5. The thinking with this order of interventions is to increase overall touch and positive attention. It is possible that these two steps could decrease the problem behaviors. Increasing quality time is also a potentially effective general intervention. So, the first two or three items on the list would be the first step. Step three would take more planning and could be helpful at some point as a form of teaching. With this step the child is getting special attention, accomplishing several interventions at once. Step five is listed last on this list because it represents the greatest risk due to the triggers that have resulted in the problem touch in the past. It is a good intervention to give a child a situation and this time helping her handle it much better than in the past. However, the results may be better if several other interventions would precede this test situation.

Now that we have a list of elements to put into a plan, it is important to operationalize what you are specifically going to do. Here are some possibilities for the first three interventions:

Intervention 1 – Increase the overall amount of touch Cheryl receives by doing any or all of the following: start her day with a big hug, each time you see her you can touch her in some way such as patting her back or asking for a 'high five,' have her sit by you to watch a TV show and hold her hand or put your arm around her during the show.

Intervention 4 – Increase Cheryl's positive attention with steps such as: go out of your way to compliment the things she does well, express particular appreciation when you find her being helpful even if you ask her to do something for you, find something she has done recently and let her know how thankful you are for her help.

Intervention 2 – Increase her quality time with key adults by: taking a walk in a park, taking a drive and talking on the way there and back, asking her what she would like to do, have some hot tea or chocolate before bedtime, play a game of Cheryl's choosing, or any number of other child centered activities.

Another important element of interventions is to never expect to succeed on the first try. In almost all cases it will take some adjustments to the interventions you are using. However, having a plan such as the one above will almost always lower the stress felt by parents because you know what you are doing and you can put your energy into action to improve a problem situation. Give your interventions ample time to see if they are helping. The suggestion is to give any intervention at least two weeks before giving up on it, this should mean that you have tried it on many occasions. When considering if an intervention worked, the measure is not if the behavior has disappeared but if the frequency has decreased. In order to know if you are getting fewer problem incidents, you must have a baseline of how often the behavior is occurring before you try any intervention. Many adults get frustrated and give up on an intervention believing it is not working because the child continued to exhibit the problem. However, with a closer look they might find that although the behavior has not disappeared, it is happening 25% or even 50% less often than it did before and, therefore, you are headed in the right direction.

Scenario #2 Interventions

Christopher has a more problematic past than Cheryl and, not surprisingly, he has a more problematic pattern of current behaviors. The first issue with Christopher that should gain your attention is the pattern of chronic neglect in his life. Neglect has the most serious long-term impacts of any kind of abuse and will often present a number of issues for adults when it comes to his behavior.

Before we go further with responding to Christopher's issues, a few comments on neglect may be helpful. Neglect has the most serious long-term impacts because it changes the way the brain perceives the world. It also generally develops an internal working model that the child's needs will not be noticed or addressed by adults, particularly parents or anyone in the role of a primary care provider. Children are extremely vulnerable to parents, and when basic needs are not met the child's brain steps in to do all it can to provide survival. The brain may develop a reactive and negative stance toward parent figures so as to not set up vulnerability or becoming dependent upon an adult again. This is because the child's brain believes the results will be the same—needs and wants will not be met. It would be wise to anticipate a number of possible outcomes due to Christopher's neglectful past. Some of these could be a lack of trust in adults, reactivity to and avoidance of following rules, lying and all forms of manipulation and gaining power over the environment and the people interacting with the child, and a negative disposition due to believing that the outcome of events will usually be negative.

It is therefore not a surprise to learn that Christopher does not like rules or following them, or that he develops a negative, moody disposition when corrected by adults. The translation of Christopher's problematic sexual behavior fits within the profile of neglect mentioned above. From the previous section discussing the translation of his behavior, the most likely statement he is making is that power and control are what he is looking for and his behavior in relationships with peers is one place he seeks to gain the upper hand by sexual acts that often intimidate other children. Clearly this is a much more serious issue than Cheryl's. It will take specific steps if

Christopher will be able to stay in public school and have other children assured the safety they deserve from intimidation and sexual acting out.

With the above understanding of what Christopher is needing and wanting (keep in mind we may be wrong or partially wrong), we can now consider a number of possible interventions. The best interventions for any problem behavior will involve all aspects of the child's life--home/school/community.

1. Once again the most successful intervention to reduce or eliminate sexual behavior is with close adult supervision. Therefore, Christopher must be closely monitored when he is with peers. This will be particularly important at school where he has significant contact with peers.

2. Young people with a past similar to Christopher's often respond well to mentoring relationships. Giving him time with a supportive adult who is not in the role of a disciplinarian, like the adults at home and school, may be an effective step to take.

3. Find an adult-mediated youth activity program. Parents are often reluctant to have children like Christopher participate in activities outside the home because of concern about it going badly. However, more not less positive activity with peers is often a better direction for struggling children.

4. Set up a check-in person at school. Many schools have a counselor or social worker who could spend just a few minutes a couple times a week with Christopher to let him know they care about how he is doing at school. Although it is best that this person not be the teacher, who is in a quasi-parent role at school, it could be an aide or even someone on the maintenance staff.

5. Get professional help for Christopher before he is involved in serious behavior. With his background it is a good idea to find a therapist with experience with neglected children and the many predictable consequences that are often present with these children. It may help to have a time each week where Christopher is the center of an adult's attention—where he is not required to study or do chores and he can simply be himself.

Looking at this short list of possible interventions, the list could be much longer but is intentionally brief, the suggestion in Christopher's situation would be to start with two or three from the above list. For discussion sake, the recommendation would be to go in this order: 1 – 5 – 3 – 2 – 4. He will need close supervision at school, particularly in the transition times and non-classroom times such as before and after school, lunch, recess, in the hallways and in the restroom. It will be important to work with the school staff to bring him to school and hand him off from one adult to another adult and have close monitoring at the other times. Generally school staff are supportive in these cases, but if they resist the "extra work" then point out the extra work involved in lawsuits from parents of children who are sexually touched by a child known to be a concern and was not closely supervised.

Children like Christopher should always have some contact with a professional. A trained therapist can not only prevent problems but also can provide a check-in as to how the child is doing with their thinking and their emotions and offer guidance on what adults can do to further help him. Youth activities such as scouting, youth sports, church youth groups, etc. are a good way to help Christopher feel more included with others in a focused way. The adults in the program will need to know that Christopher has had a difficult childhood, and he will need extra attention and supervision. If you find the right adult who can be patient, understanding and positive, helping children like Christopher is often the reason they volunteer in the first place. Mentoring programs can be excellent, but a frequent challenge is the lack of enough adult mentors, and thus children are often waiting to be assigned. Having a check-in person at school can also be a good step, but it could be something added as the plan proceeds. It is not a good idea to try many interventions all at once. Helping children with abusive histories is a long-term task and adults need to move carefully, but consistently, in the direction of helping the child improve problem behavior.

Scenario #3 Interventions

Johnathan has some similarities to our other two children, but he also has some differences. He has a history of chronic neglect with a mother who has been involved in drugs and he has been in the foster care system, like Christopher. There is a reason to question if Johnathan has had some exposure to sexual behavior, although there is no confirmation. Research has found that there is a correlation between being away from the mother for long or even short periods of time and sexual abuse. Like Christopher, Johnathan was removed from his mother while she was in drug rehab. He is young, like Cheryl, but has a more problematic past than she had. One of the differences between Johnathan and our other two children is his potential exposure to the influences of drugs and/or alcohol. Unfortunately, drug and alcohol exposure is not unusual for children in foster care or children who have been adopted. There is no question that he has been impacted by his mother's use of drugs that resulted in chronic neglect. What is unknown and should be considered, is whether he had prenatal drug exposure or substance abuse neurological impacts.

It is common for children who have mothers with substance abuse problems, as well as children living in poverty, to have unclear prenatal histories. Medical professionals have struggled with diagnosing fetal alcohol effects or alcohol related neurological disorder when there is little evidence of exposure to drugs and alcohol. However, for our purposes it is wise to consider the possibility of early drug or alcohol exposure when considering interventions for children like Johnathan, regardless of whether there is factual evidence.

Johnathan has shown himself to be a risk of sexual behavior, and involving other children in such behavior. When considering a number of possible translations, it was determined that the best fit was normative sex play rather than more serious signs of behavioral or emotional disturbance. Johnathan was added to the children in these examples to reflect that even when a child has a problematic past and potential exposure to drugs or alcohol during prenatal development, this does not immediately determine disturbed behavior. In this case, the initial hypothesis (that could turn out to be incorrect) is that he is reflecting behavior that is normative for his age and development.

It will be good to keep in mind the neglect and possible exposure to sexual behavior and the potential of drug and alcohol exposure, but we will begin by developing interventions that address normative themes at Johnathan's age and situation.

1. Adults must closely monitor Johnathan's contact with other children in the preschool and elsewhere. Step one would be to work with preschool staff to allow him to continue in the program with a heightened level of supervision.
2. Increase the amount of physical touch Johnathan receives in all settings. The combination of touch being

a basic need and the neglect in his past would make this a very good preventative step.

3. Increase the amount of play in Johnathan's environment. Normative sex play is exactly what the term says—it is play. Although you do not want Johnathan to play doctor, the 'penis game' (any activity centered around penises), or the let's discover what is under our clothing game, these are all normative activities for children Johnathan's age. It is important to increase play in other areas if you decrease sex play.

4. Reduce the amount of anxiety Johnathan is experiencing. Although we do not have information that Johnathan is having high levels of stress, sex play can be a symptom of a need for stress release. A good method to reduce stress in young children is to increase the predictable structure around him. Suggestions include: consistent bedtimes, meal times when he expects them, and other steps to calm his brain that could still be struggling with the impacts of early neglect.

5. Involve Johnathan in high energy group games with his peers. Johnathan is a child who enjoys playing and having contact with his peers. High energy games may help with stress, with making contact with others and with having fun. There is play that is more fun than sex play, so find out what this may be for him.

Based upon what we know about Johnathan, the recommended plan would be to proceed in this order: 1 – 4 – 2 – 3 – 5. Supervision is a critically important first step. After this step there are interventions that must be monitored to see if they address the problem. Will reducing his stress cut down on the frequency of the problem? Will increasing physical touch help? These are questions that need to be answered. Be prepared to adjust both what does not work and what partially works to increase the effectiveness.

When you take the time to translate the behavior of a child to learn more about his or her inner world, there are times that interventions may seem to have nothing to do with the problem behavior. But if the intervention addresses a deeper need, it may just achieve the improvement you are looking for.

Although there are some similarities with the above examples, there will always be differences with children and unique aspects of the child's past or differences in how the child responds to your interventions or events in the environment. No two children will respond in the same way, so avoid the trap some adults get into when they have had success in the past and assume the same approach will work with all children.

Generic interventions

General themes of effective interventions with young people will include: increasing positive attention, increasing supervision, providing more predictable structure and increasing the amount of fun and enjoyment. Regardless of the problematic issue, whether sexual or not, interventions that address these themes are a good start, particularly if you are not sure what to do next.

Why 'The Sex Talk' Is Ineffective

Now that specific examples have been provided for a process to arrive at interventions, our topic moves back to how parents can promote sexual health. Some parents mistakenly believe that once they have given children sexual information in the sex talk that they have fulfilled their obligation. As with every other form of learning with children, once is never enough and children do not learn what they need to understand from instruction alone. Teachers don't explain the alphabet once and call it good, coaches don't explain the rules of soccer and then put a child into the game. Learning comes from many sources, the least of which is explanations from adults.

The first inclination of parents when facing sexual issues with children is not to add gasoline to the fire by bringing up the topic of sex. Research has found that when adults provide sexual information, this does not increase sexual behavior (Baldo, Aggleton, & Slutkin 1993). Actually, when parents notice children having sexual curiosity, this is a great time to address the topic of sexuality—not in a one-time sex talk but over time and using opportunities in everyday life to integrate sex into the child's life and not setting it apart. The goal is to give children the message that sex is not dirty and secretive, but a part of who we are and adults are the best source of learning more about sexuality.

There are other problems with the one-time sex talk being helpful. Most parents do not see themselves as experts or particularly knowledgeable about sex, so they go into detailed discussions with little confidence that they will do a good job. Without confidence the tension level goes up, which is picked up by the child and everyone senses the anxiety. Under these conditions, the adult and the child want the experience to be over as soon as possible. Contrast this with a natural conversation between a parent and child about some aspect of sexuality that comes up in the child's everyday experience, is discussed briefly and without tension, and the adult and child move on to other topics.

The capacity of a child to stay focused on a topic depends upon factors such as age, interest and presence of distractions to name a few, but few children can get through a detailed sex talk without getting bored and wanting it to end. This in itself limits the amount of learning for the children and sets a tone of disliking talking about sexuality with the adult because it just isn't fun.

The primary point is that sexuality is not the polio vaccine where one inoculation addresses the problem for the foreseeable future. Sex is a topic more like learning to communicate with others, there are many complex issues children need to learn and there is always more to learn when situations come up.

Resources that Can Help Teach Children Healthy Views of Sexuality

In addition to this book, there are many resources available to parents and any adult who wants to help a child better understand sex and promote healthy sexuality. Some resources are better than others. A couple that will be mentioned here are a non-profit organization and governmental organization.

The non-profit organization, with over thirty years of experience, is Advocates for Youth which works nationally and internationally supporting sexual health among young people. The following are suggestions coming from this organization that are consistent with other suggestions in this book:

- ✓ Examine your own beliefs and values before teaching a child.
- ✓ Assert your own personal privacy boundaries, decline to discuss private sexual behavior.
- ✓ Use accurate language for body parts and functions.

✓ Discuss sexuality at times that work best for connecting with your child.
✓ Clarify relationships and how people are related to others.
✓ Use photos, pictures and visual materials.
✓ Use teachable moments that come up in daily life.
✓ Be honest in answering questions.
✓ Value the child's feelings and experience.
✓ Offer praise and support.
✓ Repeat information over time, as needed.
✓ Take advantage of available resources.

Advocates for Youth
http://www.advocatesforyouth.org/parents/

The second is a governmental organization called Healthfinder.gov which is a division of the United States Department of Health and Human Services. This resource covers not only talking to your child about healthy sexuality, but also covers healthy relationships. Here are some suggestions from this organization:

• Talk early and often – you don't have to fit everything into one conversation.
• Be ready to answer questions. Your child's questions can tell you a lot about what she already knows.
• Listen carefully to your child, even if you don't agree with his opinion.
• Try using examples from TV or music to start a conversation.
• Be honest about how you are feeling. For example, if you are embarrassed or uncomfortable, it's okay to say so.
• Develop skills for healthy and safe relationships.

- Set expectations for how the young person wants to be treated.
- Recognize when a relationship doesn't feel good.

Healthfinder.gov also considers the question--what is a healthy relationship? Sexuality is closely connected to relationships, and here are components of a relationship that are positive for both individuals:

- Both people feel respected, supported and valued.
- Decisions are made together.
- Both people have friends and interests outside of the relationship.
- Disagreements are settled with open and honest communication.
- There are more good times than bad.
- One person does not try to change the other.
- One person does not make most or all of the decisions.
- One or both individuals do not drop friends and interests outside of the relationship.
- Neither person yells, threatens, hits or throws things during arguments.
- One person does not make fun of the other's opinions or interests.
- Neither person keeps track of the other all the time by calling, texting or checking in with friends.

http://healthfinder.gov/FindServices/SearchContext.aspx?topic=783

What If My Child Thinks She or He Is Lesbian or Gay?

Any book on helping children with sexuality must address to some degree the lesbian, gay, bi-sexual, transsexual and asexual areas of sexual attraction (or lack of attraction). Few areas of sexuality are currently as controversial in our society as issues such as gay rights, gay marriage and tolerance for sexual minority groups. Clearly our society is having the turmoil in the area of sexual minorities that it had in the 1960s with dominant sexual themes. In the news each day, conflicts seem to be heating up rather than cooling off. One thing is sure, our current society is not the same as a couple generations ago when it comes to societal views of sexuality. As the centenarian comic George Burns once noted, "I can remember when the air was clean and sex was dirty."

Not long ago sexual minority groups were defined as reflecting mental illness, and there were essentially universal laws against homosexual behavior. Mainstream psychiatry no longer considers gay preference to be a mental disturbance that needs treatment, but there are still ample laws throughout our society concerning homosexual behavior and lifestyle issues. In other countries of the world the struggle for gay rights is not too different than what was going on in the United States a few decades ago, such as the attention on Russian anti-gay laws highlighted by the 2014 Sochi Winter Olympics or the persecution of gays in several countries on the African continent.

With society still in flux when it comes to perceptions of sexual minorities, how is a parent to handle sexual interests that are not part of our current dominant sexual values and lifestyle choices? There are no easy answers to help parents who run into these issues for the first time. The one principle that helps is that regardless of what children believe at certain ages about their sexual preferences, the advice to parents is that everything in this book applies to these children as well — model respect, do your best to take the emotional reactivity out of the issue, support the child, teach clear boundaries, promote open communication and all the other principles that have been covered here. In modern times it seems that every generation has brought challenges of a sexual nature to their elders and this continues today, as it will continue tomorrow. Like any other issue, sexual behavior and sexual lifestyles cannot be separated from our value systems. If you are honest with your child, you will need to be open with your beliefs and moral principles. Children cannot be raised in a moral vacuum. However, remember that your job as a parent is to at some point put yourself out of the role of being your child's moral compass. Morality must be internalized at some point, and the parent can help by allowing the child to develop personal values and moral principles he or she can carry into the future as the drive toward independence progresses.

Promoting Sexual Health for Children Who Have Been Sexually Abused

There is one population of children where the topic of sexual health is often ignored — children who have been sexually abused. This is a travesty and it must be addressed. Otherwise there is an entire population of children who will grow up equating sex with pain and victimization. There are many rationalizations for ignoring healthy sexuality with this population but none justify putting the child in the position of losing the opportunity to develop positive sexual health.

The results of sexual trauma have been widely communicated in our society. Most adults and children know that sexual abuse is bad and can produce serious long-term problems. An extensive discussion of the negative impacts of sexual trauma will not be provided here, but it is essential to understand that extensive efforts may be required to overcome the negative impacts of sexual trauma if a healthy perception of sex is to be achieved. Here are only some of the barriers to sexual health after trauma:

- Betrayal of trust produces mistrustful inner working model. Children can generalize fear of sexual trauma from the perpetrator to others.
- Hypersensitivity to sexual themes. The child may turn everyday situations into something sexual.
- Avoidance of adults who want something. The child's brain fears further victimization and reacts to what adults want.
- Sexualizing motivation and behavior of others. Some children experience fear of others when there is no reason to be concerned.
- Loss of correctly understanding the interests and messages of others. When the child is trying to avoid vulnerability, he or she may miss the message being communicated.
- Excessive self-protection. The child may put up walls where they are not needed or helpful and important relationships can be damaged.
- Avoidance of intimacy and vulnerability. Sexual trauma can produce distancing from others and pushing away healthy relationships.
- Excessive need for control. Feeling powerless resulting in abuse can lead to an intense need to manage others and the environment.

- Fear of the internal drive to join with a love interest. It is healthy to love and to trust, but how does a child do this after being victimized?

Often adults believe that the best thing to do is to create an asexual world for the child so sexual triggers are not present. Following sexual abuse, many children are hypersensitive to sexual issues and adults believe it helps the child to stay away from aspects of sexuality. Because some traumatized children have increased sexually reactive behavior, adults mistakenly believe that discussing healthy sexuality will increase sexual behavior, but research does not support this belief (Baldo, Aggleton & Slutkin, 1993). Other mistaken beliefs have also prompted adults to have children who have experienced sexual trauma to live in an environment where sex is ignored. Adults believe that children who are sexually abused often become abusers themselves, but this may be the case for only half of one percent (Friedrich & Chaffin, 2000; Johnson, 1998; Widom, 1994). While it is important to recognize the potential damage of sexual abuse, there has often been an overestimation of the long-term damage caused by sexual trauma (Friedrich, 2002; Kendall-Tackett, Williams & Finkelhor, 1993) that has caused some adults to attempt to remove any elements of sex from the child's development. Regardless of the reasons that adults believe avoiding the issue of healthy sexuality with sexually abused children, it is not a good idea for a population that needs help to develop healthy sexual thoughts, feelings and behaviors even more than children who have not been sexually abused.

Even more unfortunate is how the professional community has failed to address healthy sexuality for sexually abused children. Among professionals, nearly all the attention goes to healing the psychological damage of sexual trauma. Focusing on healing does make sense but what is the child left with after trauma therapy regarding perceptions of sex? What positive role can it play in life after very negative sexual experiences? What does the child do with sexual feelings and desires, and many other similar matters? Unfortunately the message most adults give sexually abused children is the familiar 'just say no to sex,' and this is usually for the best interests of the adult, not the child.

Nearly twenty years ago I was discussing the need to help sexually abused children gain a more healthy view of sex with Jan Hindman, who has been mentioned previously. We agreed to put some energy into this area and at some point perhaps collaborate in writing a book on the subject. A collaborative effort never happened but we both did give this topic some much needed focus in our individual work. Jan would go on to write a book on the general topic of sexuality called *There is No Sex Fairy*, a title only Jan would come up with (Hindman, 2007). On my end, I developed the first college course in the US on the topic of promoting healthy sexuality after sexual abuse and taught the course for many years at Portland State University. A recent search on both Google and Bing came up with only one reference to promoting healthy sexuality in children after sexual abuse and that was my own work. So unfortunately, little has changed over the years on this important topic.

Anyone reading this book probably does not question the need for a child to get help to develop a healthy sense of sexuality after being victimized in a sexual way. But just in case the need is unclear, there are several reasons why this topic and this population go together perfectly. The most typical aftermath of any type of trauma is avoidance of any reminders of the negative experience — nearly drowning often results in avoidance of the water, a serious car accident can lead to fear of driving, and being seriously bitten by a dog can lead to avoidance of all dogs. We do not want the millions of children who have unfortunately been sexually abused to live a life avoiding sexuality. Even if the child does not avoid sex and perhaps is more attracted to it after sexual abuse, what is the nature of the attraction? It is probably not a healthy attraction, but closer to an interest in a taboo subject linked to something hurtful involving power and control over another person.

Children who have been sexually abused often have increased conflicts around sex, more questions, more fears of becoming someone who would do to others what was done to them and these children have often received the message to move on from sex and get it entirely out of their mind. However, childhood is a time of life when it is healthy to have curiosity and questions about sex. Sexually abused children have been taught very unhealthy messages from perpetrators — sex is a way to gain power over someone, sex is dirty, it is bad but feels good, it is secretive, and many other perceptions that a child should not take into adult years. For all these reasons, sexually abused children need our help to develop a healthy perspective even more than other children do.

Every aspect of this book is equally relevant to children who have been sexually abused as well as children who have not. However it is even more essential with traumatized children to work to alter the perception from sex being negative to sex being a positive aspect of life. How to do this is a challenge because what is required is a change in the brain's fundamental perceptions, and thoughts are directly influenced by past experiences. Perceptions are often automatic and are not the subject of higher order reasoning. If the last three Spanish teachers were kind and helpful, this helps develop a perception of all Spanish teachers, if your last two supervisors were demanding and unfair, this may develop immediate perceptions of future supervisors. To change automatic negative perceptions of sex (and any other topic), we must impact the prefrontal cortex and we must encourage a thoughtful consideration of the topic. Not all Spanish teachers are wonderful and not all supervisors are unfair, but these conclusions will only be reached by thoughtful consideration. It is not only possible to impact the perceptions of children, it is actually hard not to.

Healthy sexuality after sexual trauma is possible

The take away message is that all children deserve to have a life where sexuality is a positive component and can provide happiness and the many important benefits sexuality can bring. Do not shy away from promoting healthy perceptions and healthy information about sex with children who have been sexually abused. While this can be tricky and you may need some outside help and insight along the way, remember you are helping to give back to the child what has been robbed from them—a perception that sex is natural, good and an important part of everyone.

Transforming Perceptions of Sex from Something Bad to Good

Children develop thoughts, impressions and perceptions from the world around them, which is referred to as the nurture in the nature/nurture paradigm. This is why modeling is the most powerful form of learning, children learn what they see and experience from those around them. Following sexual abuse there is work to do in removing the negative experience of being used for someone's sexual gratification, however a negative experience in life should not be allowed to rob someone of future pleasure. A negative experience at a restaurant should not prevent someone from going out to eat, and a bad date night should not keep someone from trying again with the same person or someone else. Of course these examples are not analogous to sexual abuse but perhaps they can make a point—we should not allow someone who robs us in one situation from continuing to rob us of something good into the future.

Throughout this book practical examples and suggestions have been offered. The following will be some of the final thoughts to turn a negative issue in the past into a positive topic moving forward — sexual abuse to healthy sexuality.

Start Early

Be vigilant as to how much interest the child has in sex - this was previously called monitoring the child's focus on sexuality. It is possible to have too much or too little interest in sex. Promote a balance of interest.

Address appropriate curiosity in sexual biology – after sexual abuse the child's brain develops hypersensitivity to themes involving sex. The child will be closely looking at the reaction of adults if they ask a question about sex or other sexual themes. If the adult is not able to non-emotionally handle such a test then the child may end up with a confirmation that sex is indeed bad.

Start young to address sexual issues before you have to react to problematic behavior – when possible start young to normalize sexual issues. But, at any age, initiate discussions and information before you are in the difficult role of handling problem sexual behavior.

Integrate the child's experience in your teaching, "If anyone tries to use bad touch like before, be sure to let me know" – the message of rescue is critically important to a child who has experienced sexual trauma. Some of these children may not have experienced responsive adults, and they need to know that someone is there who cares and will come to their aid.

Model respect with all family members – like everything else you want the child to learn, respect is learned best through modeling. Your entire family needs to treat all family members with respect and, if they don't, the child needs to see that you will step in and rectify any lack of respect.

Avoid requiring abused children to hug, kiss and touch people they prefer not to touch – here is an area of controversy for some adults. If Aunt Margaret loves to kiss little Jill and be kissed in return then does Jill have any say in the matter? This issue becomes even more worthy of consideration if Jill has been on the receiving end of having her boundaries intruded upon without her consent. If you put yourself in the child's shoes, the decision should be clear.

You need to be the primary source of sexual information

Children are always learning, so what are they learning about sex? Consider the child's sources of information: TV, movies, video games, older children and music, to name a few influences. If you are to make the positive impact you want to then you must be a major source of information about the positive aspects of sexuality.

A sexually abused child in a sexualized society

In Part I the point was made that our society is far from healthy when it comes to sexuality. For a moment, consider what it must be like to have experienced sexual victimization that developed a hypersensitivity to sex with all the sexual triggers previously discussed—TV, movies, magazines, music, outdoor advertising, videogames, the internet, the list goes on and on. How does the child develop a sense of safety and normalcy in a culture seemingly out of control with sexual themes. There are no easy answers, but we must put ourselves in the shoes of the child to understand the challenge they face and need help with.

126

Another reminder, the goal is healthy sexual interest, not no sexual interest – if a child is too focused on sex, particularly in unhealthy ways, or if a child shows no overt interest in sex, then your task is to present a well-adjusted and healthy balance of interest concerning sexual issues.

You must correct the many distorted experiences the child has from past sexual abuse – it is very possible that the child has been told very negative messages about sex, that it is evil, the child is bad because he or she was involved in something bad, the devil will come get children who think sexual thoughts, and many other very negative and unhealthy things. If you do not provide messages that contradict this negativity, the child is left with the uncorrected result of past abuse and is further disadvantaged.

Rules, Robbery and Rescue

These are three important areas for sexually abused children. For some of these children the experience they have gone through may have violated each of these areas. Rules for personal boundaries are to be followed by everyone, even adults. If someone robs you, it is not right and they are responsible and not you. Finally, rescue is available at any time, all you have to do is ask for help. After an experience where the three R's are violated, what is left is a child who needs a great deal of reassurance over time.

Go over rules of touching, space, and consent – many abused children are not aware of rules when it comes to touch and they need instruction and supervision. The concept of the personal space that others deserve is often foreign to these children. Consent is an essential concept for all young people and even more so for the child who was not asked for his or her consent when they were abused. This consent is not the legal term where children are not mature enough to consent to business agreements, research or sexual contact. This consent means the child has a voice and with that voice agrees to be involved.

Use the language of playing games, "We don't play the penis touching game in our home" – this concept can help parents who are not very comfortable talking about sexual matters (that would be most of us). For young children, put sexual behavior into the language of play. When the adult is more comfortable, the child is more likely to hear the content of the message rather than the non-verbal discomfort of the messenger.

Teach the child that our bodies are like our other important possessions, we care for them and protect them – Jan Hindman often said to children, "Your body is like a new bicycle—it is important that you care for it, protect it, and not let others scratch or damage it and your body is even more valuable than a new bike."

Don't keep the child from the world, give the child the ability to make good choices.

The child may have already found the dangers, help the child know the good from the bad.

Teach critical thinking, "In this story who was right and who was wrong?"

Explain to the child the dangers, don't pretend they don't exist.

Explain to the child the people and places to avoid and why.

Don't teach fear, teach safety and encourage good decision-making.

Equality and Personal Value

Rights and equality are very important for sexually abused children to learn. Your home must be a place where the child sees the modeling of gender equality. Everyone does not do the same things in the family but everyone is equal.

Children must feel they have a place and a voice in the family or they may experience being a victim again.

Teach consent in all matters, so the child will understand the concept with touching. Did Dustin give you permission to play with that? You must ask Janah if you want to read her book. Private things are those that others do not have permission to see.

The Ten Year Rule

Are all these areas really that important for sexually abused children? Perhaps not all are essential in the short run, but everything you are doing to help the child is developing a sense of self, learning rules to live by and being taught the rights of others, is preparing the child for the future. Practice the Ten Year Rule, what does this child need to learn today to be successful in ten years? Adults should always be thinking not only about the present, but how to prepare the child for the future.

A Special Emphasis on Respect

Respect has been stressed throughout this book and sexually abused children can be a challenge because they may not respect you, others or themselves. The golden rule (treat others as you wish to be treated in return) is of little use if you don't respect yourself or care how you are treated.

Make sure your home is a place of respect among everyone, if not, the child must experience you requiring it of everyone.

Respect is first learned in other areas before it is understood with sexuality – boundaries, rules, consent can all be learned by children in everyday activities. Make sure the concept is clear before applying it to sexuality.

You must specifically teach respecting boundaries to children who have had their private space violated – with sexually abused children there is some unlearning to be done.

Be patient, it takes time to teach something that is not automatic – few of the concepts covered here are found in the animal kingdom because they require higher levels of thought and behavior. Humans are animals and higher aspirations must rise above primitive patterns of behavior.

Resiliency and Responsibility

Help children separate who they are from what was done to them – counter the self-perception that since the child was involved in something bad, then the child is bad.

Realize that many abused children have negative views of self and the future. You may need to alter both – perceptions are important but so are negative thoughts about the future, further victimization and a life of isolation and unhappiness. Such negative thoughts can become self-fulfilling prophecies.

Teach children how to bounce back from adversity – this is resiliency and it requires that someone believe in the child and their ability to rise above difficult circumstances. Children can learn resiliency by overcoming small things first and thus finding some success, and then bouncing back from bigger things.

Point out when children overcome difficult problems and reinforce successes – find situations where the child did well and bring it to the attention of the child. Negative self-perceptions of traumatized children often disregard successes and positive accomplishments, don't let that happen!

Self-Control, Delaying Gratification and Positive Self Esteem

Delaying gratification does not come naturally, teach the child what can be gained by waiting for later. This is a principle in so many aspects of life: education, career, financial investment, relationship building and goal-setting. Start small and build to larger issues when teaching this concept.

Connect delaying gratification with internal control, children love to be in control. One universal characteristic of traumatized children is their need for control. Help the child see that control of self is the most important control they will ever achieve.

Build the inner self of the child whenever possible – in all interactions with the child, including correcting the child's behavior, there is an opportunity to let the child know that you believe he or she can succeed.

We act in ways that are consistent with how we view ourselves, improve the child's inner self-view. Most children who view themselves as a bad person often act badly. Positive self-perceptions often are reflected in positive behavior.

Protecting the Vulnerable, Making Amends to Others and How Guilt can be Positive

Respect covers many issues, start wherever the child is in teaching it. Respect things such as toys or electronics. Respect for nature. Respect for family members, even those the child does not get along with. Respect for peers, adults and strangers all must be taught.

Teach children to help, not take advantage of, more vulnerable animals and people. The theme of helping, not hurting, the vulnerable goes against the animal nature of people. The vulnerable of any member of the animal kingdom do not fare well. Taking advantage of vulnerability of all kinds must turn into protecting the vulnerable.

There is a good aspect of shame and guilt, it is knowing you have not done your best and you have not listened to your conscience—your internal moral compass. Individuals who hurt others without remorse need some healthy shame and guilt to do better the next time.

When was the last time you apologized to a child?

Why do many adults expect children to know how to apologize for something they have done wrong? Taking responsibility and apologizing do not come naturally. Denying, defending and doing anything to protect yourself by getting out of a difficult situation—these come naturally. How do children learn the very important social skill of accepting responsibility and apologizing to someone else? The best method is modeling. You use polite words around children so they will learn to do the same, you use good manners for the same reason. So find a reason to apologize to a child so they learn from example, otherwise where will they learn it?

Teach the child to fix what they break—apologize, agree not to repeat the harm, and make amends. This goes back to how children learn best—modeling. Start by using opportunities to apologize to the child. An apology includes several steps: taking responsibility, saying you are sorry and meaning it, making restitution and making a commitment not to do the same thing again. An apology that misses any of these steps is not sufficient.

The "golden rule" is the best anti-bullying plan. Most everyone hates to be bullied, if a child can learn to understand treating others as you wish to be treated, then this is a great anti-bullying message.

Touch and Caring Should Always Go Together

Sexuality is an extension of many aspects of life—respect, caring, intimacy, equality and consideration.

Reframe the meaning of touch, particularly caring and loving touch. To a child who has been touched in an abusive way, a positive perception of this basic need must be stressed. Touch can be good or bad, caring or hurtful. Model and teach through experience the positive elements of touch.

Parents must be the message they want their children to understand—it is all about modeling.

Avoid touching sexually abused children!

You have heard this before—don't touch because the child will misinterpret or worse, you might be falsely accused of abuse. It is understandable where this concern comes from, but that does not make it a good idea. Not only do traumatized children need touch, they need it more than non-traumatized children. There may be a lot of bad touch to make up for, there may be years of unmet needs for supportive touch. The body also needs to learn new body memories that contact with another person is not hurtful. Touch in the right way, at the right time, with the child's consent, but please touch!

Suggestions for Parents of Sexually Abused Children

If you are raising a child who has been sexually abused at some point in their childhood, you know how difficult it can be. The job of being a parent is considered by many the most difficult job on the planet, then add to this challenge doing the most difficult job with a child who has experienced sexual trauma and it feels like 'mission impossible.' If you are finding it difficult to parent the child, much less promote healthy sexuality, you are not alone and you are finding it difficult for very good reasons. Here are a few suggestions for you:

First, focus on developing a healthy connection with the child – sexual health must take a back seat to first developing a close connection with the child. Without this foundation, the trust needed for so much of what we have covered will be beyond your reach. Every situation can be grist for the mill of a deeper relationship with the child, even problems, even conflicts and even the tough times.

Separating the child from the behavior – while it is not easy to parent the child, it is even more difficult for the child to function after something as terrible as sexual abuse. When the child acts out or makes major mistakes, take the time to remember the needy child behind the unacceptable behavior. Many traumatized children can say and do very unpleasant things when they experience significant stress. If you are the target of this, do not take it personally because it is almost never solely about you, regardless of what the child may say to upset you.

Being a good listener – there are many times in life that we cannot change what has happened. This is true for sexual abuse, you cannot take back the abuse. At these times, one of the best things you can do is to be truly present with the child and listen. Listen not just to the child's words, but also to what he or she is really saying to you. A good listener is easy to talk to, is not distracted or in a hurry, is not judgmental and lets the child know that you are interested in what is being said regardless of the content. Even if the child is telling a story that has little meaning to you, listening says 'I care about you' which is the most important message you can give the child.

Saying no with love – there is no question that a victimized child hurts the heart of all caring adults. However, being sensitive to the child and being easy on the child are two very different things. Traumatized children do not need adults acting in ways that reflect feeling sorry for them and, therefore, not holding the child accountable. This can teach the child to use their former abuse in a manipulative way. Traumatized children need structure, rules, schedules, predictability and do not need adults to let them get away with behavior other children cannot do. It can be difficult at times to say no, particularly when it would be easy to say yes, but the child needs a firm parent to feel safe. Practice saying no with love in small and big matters. This includes not letting the child do what he or she wants when it is not best for the child.

Correctly understanding the child's needs and then meet these needs – what do sexually abused children need? The starting place is what every child needs: love, touch, safety, physical and emotional nourishment, to belong, to express thoughts and feelings, to play and to learn. Sexually abused children need the very same things, but they need these needs met to an even greater degree and may need to have needs met somewhat differently. The closer you get to the child's inner world, the better you will be able to know how to best meet the child's most important needs.

Forming a team with the therapist, teacher and others in the child's life – it is not a good idea to do your difficult job alone, get help from others. All the adults in the child's life should be on the same page. Therefore, connect with these adults — the child's teacher, mentor, therapist, coach, pastor, relatives, neighbors and any other adults who interact with the child.

Suggestions for Professionals in Helping Families with Childhood Sexual Behavior

Families play the most important role for children to both heal from any trauma including sexual trauma and to develop healthy sexuality. But many families have little experience or knowledge of how to help a child heal from trauma or develop sexual health because these are complex tasks. Professionals need to be prepared to help, but some actions in other situations may not be helpful to families struggling with the sexual issues of their child. So how can therapists, teachers, pastors and others be most helpful to the family?

We can start with the guiding principle that what the family does or does not do for the child at home will be much more impactful than what takes place in your office. Therefore, the child will be best helped if the family can become a therapeutic agent in the process of change and improvement. Many parents believe their role is to get the child to the 'expert' and wait for good things to happen. However, the professional's job is to coach the parent to do the most important work at home because the necessary conditions of safety, predictability, belonging and the source of support and all basic needs is the family. All these conditions are essential for physical and emotional healing. Because of the importance of what happens at home, parents will be much more influential in the progress of the child than a professional, regardless of how hard you work or how experienced you are.

Coaching parents to be therapeutic agents involves many of the same skills that are taught in good graduate programs for therapists. How to listen on a deeper level includes what is behind the words, what non-verbal messages are being said and reading the energy of the person you are listening to. Listening includes 'active listening' to encourage the child (or adult) to open up and express what it is important and perhaps difficult to communicate. Active listening means to let the individual know you understand through attention, clarifying questions, reflecting what you are hearing and summarizing what is being said. One of the most important ways to support the child is to be present, attentive and give your full attention, which can be difficult and perhaps not always characteristic of the pattern of communication between parent and child.

To be present to understand and help the child can be a shift for many parents from the teaching role to the learning role. They are not instructing or telling the child what to do, the goal in this interaction is to be led by the child rather than lead the child. The very process of a parent who is present, interested and allows the child to communicate freely has strong therapeutic benefits for the child. You may need to coach the parent in how to do this, do some role-playing because some of these skills may be new to the parent. Armed with more confidence to be a true therapeutic agent for their child can give a great deal back to the parent as well.

At times parents think it is supportive to the child who has been traumatized to be flexible with rules and structure, but often the child needs the safety and comfort of a predictable environment, and the parent provides this. While it is important to be flexible, there are good times and also the wrong times to do so. Help the parent see that being rigid is not experienced as support by the child. Rigidity says that the rules are more important than the people living with the rules. This requires a balance because flexibility with daily structure is seldom a good idea when it reduces rather than enhances predictable structure. Often, traumatized children will use their situation to push for more of what they want rather than what they need, which requires the parent to be able to say no with love. Coach parents to see when a child is pushing to test the limits of the structure and the importance of the child experiencing the parent providing the safety of this structure.

When a parent seeks help from a professional, many will do so with a sense that they have failed at something they are expected to be able to do. This is one reason why some parents are hypersensitive to the message that it is not the child but the parent who is the problem. At the point parents ask for professional help, many have become overwhelmed by the difficulty and complexity of understanding and helping their child. What these parents need to hear is just how difficult a job they have been trying to do, and why approaching the problem differently and not trying harder is the best direction to go. Parents need help to become more resilient and learn how to cope with a child who is not going to be 'cured' anytime soon.

At times, parents face the 'Sophie's Choice' of choosing the child of concern over their other children who may not be doing well themselves with the family dynamics. This is an impossible situation for the parent and the best interests of all family members must be considered. You cannot take away the dilemma but you can support the parent who faces tough choices and help them make thoughtful and not reactive decisions.

If you are able to provide the parents some reassurance that they are doing their best with a difficult situation, you may be better able to communicate important new perspectives about the situation. The first is to help the parent see any negative hypersensitivity that has developed. The irony is that if any parent needs hope and the ability to see at least small progress and positive successes, it is the parent of the children discussed throughout this book. However, what can develop is an unhelpful belief that things are not going to improve and then finding 'confirmatory bias' by spotting any evidence that supports this negative position. The second trap that you must help the parent see is becoming increasingly punitive due to desperation. The desperation is understandable and at times there is no question the child deserves a punitive response, but the problem is that a negative approach will not only probably fail, it can make the problems worse for the child and parent as well. It will take considerable skill on the part of the professional to support the parent, by letting them know that they are facing difficult issue with their child and the parent is not the problem, while also helping the parent avoid negative traps along the way.

A helpful measure is to determine if the parent has the ability to continue to find some humor and enjoyment within the family. Ideally, the parent has not lost their sense of humor and can even periodically smile at their situation. After all, it is certainly ironic that an adoptive or foster parent, who by free choice and a thoughtful decision brought a child into the family, may wonder just what they were thinking at the time. When the result of helping a child has little resemblance to the intent, it is easy to understand why a parent would question their decision. Anyone who has lost the ability to find the humor in life, including problems, is showing signs of burn-out and needs more perspective to understand that being able to find humor in all aspects of life is necessary for personal health.

Finally, the following are general suggestions that can help professionals and parents be on the same page and develop a successful plan of action:

- *Everyone agrees on the family strengths. Parents can lose perspective when facing the stress of the very difficult job they have. Make sure they know that you see the parent's strengths.*
- *Everyone agrees on the family challenges. This goes back to an important point previously made, that unless you focus on the right problem, your interventions are unlikely to be successful.*
- *For every challenge, apply a strength. The job of a good coach is to point out what strengths can be applied to the issue at hand.*
- *Agree on what positive change will look like. What is the goal and how will the parents know when they achieve it, this goes back to having perspective on the situation.*
- *Put your plan in writing. A well-developed plan often immediately reduces the stress of 'We just don't know what*

to do.' A written plan makes it more solid and it can be referred to along the way.

- Throughout the process check the respect meter. Make sure your relationship with the parent(s) retains the necessary ingredients for success on both ends – trust, listening, honesty, attention to detail and, most of all, respect.

- Give the parent the choice of what issues to work on first, second and third. There are usually many issues that need attention, give the parent the choice of starting with a major issue, or better yet, a smaller issue to have some success.

- You bring the process, the parent brings the ideas, the investment and takes the credit. Always work to put yourself out of a job with the parent feeling the confidence to handle their own challenges. Therefore, facilitate a process and don't be quick to either give the parent solutions or accept the credit when interventions work well.

- Find the reason for every small success. First, make it clear when there is a small success, it may be more obvious to you than to the parent. Then point out the reason for the success so this can be built upon.

- Find the improvement in every setback. There will be missteps, but these are not failures if you can help the parent see what was done right and now what adjustments may produce better results.

- If you lose patience, you will begin to get in a hurry, express frustration and send the opposite messages you want to send. If parents are honest with you, and this is essential, they will bring frustrations to you, perhaps even saying you are responsible for failure. Stay patient, keep a clear perspective even in the face of conflict because you are modeling exactly what the parents need to be able to do.

- The basis for all coaching is a focus on fundamentals – be confident, be open-minded, trust in your abilities, be flexible, ask for help you may need and use all challenges of parenting as an opportunity to grow personally, regardless of the outcome.

What to Do When Nothing Seems to Work

There is nothing easy about parenting and handling sexual themes for some parents is one of the most challenging parts of the role. Most parents want to start their child off with a healthy perspective in all areas, including sexuality. However, many parents have more willingness than they have confidence in their ability to do a good job on sexual matters. So you have worried, read, consulted, perhaps even prayed, and yet you find that all your efforts are failing. Now what? The starting place is always to look for your resources at home with a partner. But, you may have already done this and it is time for outside help. Some would say to pick up the phone and get some professional help. That is one resource, depending on the available help in your community. If that is the direction you chose, many parents are not sure where to turn. Suggestions were offered at the end of Part II under "How to find the right help." Who the person is can be critically important. This is much more important than the person's discipline, degrees or methods. Do you approach a psychiatrist (a medical doctor with medication training) or a psychologist (a psychological doctor with training in psychotherapy) or a clinical social worker, family therapist, or child development professional? The choice is yours but, again, the person is much more important than the degree. So when looking for the right individual to help you, there is considerable information available on the internet to find available professionals. Just remember the quality of the website is not always indicative of the quality of the person.

But professionals are not the only resource for ideas, support and help. In fact, you may want to first start with a trusted friend. The issue may not be less that you don't know what to do than you simple need some objective support and a reality check. You may get both from a good friend, a trusted neighbor, a family member you find supportive and helpful, someone in your network of people you know at the PTA or exercise class, or someone you trust in your faith community. Remember, it is more important who the person is than what they do for a living. However, good people can have some poor ideas, so use your instincts and recognize when you are looking in the wrong place for the help you are looking for.

Is Achieving Sexual Health Possible?

We have come to the end of the discussion of promoting sexual health with children. But let's be real, with all the barriers and challenges we have discussed, is achieving sexual health even possible? Perhaps the same question could be asked about other types of health — emotional health, spiritual health, and even mental health. There is no universally acknowledged measure of any of these aspects of health. Take, for example, mental health. The most recognized measuring stick of mental health is offered by the American Psychiatric Association with their recently released DSM 5 (APA, 2013). But no sooner than the effort began to pull together the most recent version of what is considered mentally and behaviorally healthy and unhealthy, did the quarrelling begin. The DSM 5 was released in 2013 with as much criticism as support. Some of the strongest criticism has come from psychiatrists themselves, including the main authors of earlier versions of the Manual. Just one area of the criticism is if we cannot agree on what is healthy, then how can we agree on what constitutes unhealthy. Another chorus of criticism is the concern that the Manual is taking normal experiences of life and considering them pathological. So is it possible to achieve health if the experts can't agree on what is and isn't healthy?

Experts are not the only source of determining health. Certainly health is influenced by cultural definitions to a large degree. Some behaviors in the western world would be viewed by Muslim countries are not only unhealthy, but illegal and perverse. Western cultures would reply that strict Muslim countries are repressed, uptight and restricted to an unhealthy extreme. The culture we live in has definite opinions about what is healthy, even if there is a lack of consensus within the culture in some areas. Therefore health is a relative concept, its definition is influenced by many things including culture and personal values. This certainly includes sexual health. Since there is no objective measure of sexual health, a subjective measure will have to do.

Is it possible to achieve sexual health? In the end, the answer may have to be determined by the subjective measure of each individual. Like other types of health, sexual health may be viewed on a continuum where an individual is more or less healthy rather than being one or the other. There are many unhealthy ways that sex is viewed, used and practiced as we have discussed. A goal throughout life for everyone could be to work to improve sexual health as well as physical, mental and spiritual health. As the Nike ad says, "There is no finish line." So one answer to the question, is achieving sexual health possible, is that it is certainly possible to become more sexually healthy with effort, and the potential of what sexual health can add to everyone's life makes it a worthwhile goal.

As difficult as it is to promote healthy sexual development and healthy behavior with children, it is also worth the effort. Because all parents have limits to their own sexual health, it is probable that despite your best efforts you will be deficient in some respects. Like all other aspects of parenting, the goal is not perfection but doing your best. None of us had perfect parents and few of us had ideal sexual orientation and development as we grew up. Unless you specifically cause damage to a child, there is little cause to be concerned for making mistakes in parenting. We all learn by our mistakes and children can also learn from parental mistakes when parents model taking responsibility and even apologizing for mistakes. But this does not relieve a parent from the responsibility to do the very best they can to give a child the information and insight that can greatly improve aspects of the child's life. A parent that promotes healthy eating habits can greatly improve a child's physical health in the long-run. A parent who promotes spiritual health, and models this, can provide a child with a moral compass that can guide the child through the good and bad times throughout life. And the parent who does his or her very best to instill healthy sexual attitudes and behaviors is giving the child a precious gift that too few children receive.

Like all aspects of parenting, the effort you put into being the best parent you can possibly be is not just for your child. When we help or do something for someone else, we are working on ourselves at the same time. Sexual health is a great example of this principle. We started this book with a look inward at our own sexual health and we will finish with the same theme. Perhaps it would be worthwhile to return to the Sexual Health Questionnaire after reading this book and giving thought to the points that have been covered then take the test again. If you take the time to do this, did your score improve? Did your own sexual health progress, because if it did that is precisely the point—we give to our children what we possess ourselves, in this case the degree to which we ourselves have sexual health.

It is very possible that this has been a difficult topic for you to consider by reading this book, sexuality is a complex and perplexing issues for most people throughout life. I hope you see the value in giving your child a good start toward sexual health as early as possible. Congratulations on making it through this process to this point in the book, but remember there is no finish line, your child will mainly receive from you the level of health that you model. The journey of life and the journey toward sexual health are difficult, but the rewards can be great and well worth it. I wish you the very best in your efforts to promote in your child sexual health.

Summary Points

➢ Stay calm, stay vigilant and start teaching children about sexuality as young as you can.

➢ You need to be comfortable discussing sexual issues if you want your child to be comfortable.

➢ Distinguish between the child and the child's behavior; teach the child—correct the behavior.

➢ Don't overstate and don't understate how serious the child's behavior is.

➢ Get some help, raising a child is a team sport, particularly when it comes to sexual issues.

➢ Understand the meaning of the behavior or you will have unsuccessful interventions.

➢ Good information and resources are available, take advantage of them.

➢ Children who have been sexually abused are a challenge and require additional attention.

➢ Address sexual issues in the present with an eye on preparing the child for their future.

➢ Improving your own sexual health will help your child, but if not it will help you.

References

American Psychiatric Association. (2013). The Diagnostic and Statistical Manual of Mental Disorders. Arlington, VA: American Psychiatric Publishing.

Baldo, M., Aggleton, P. & Slutkin G. (1993). Does Sex Education Lead to Earlier or Increased Sexual Activity in Youth? Presented at the Ninth International Conference on AIDS, Berlin, 6-10. Geneva: World Health Organization, 1993.

Beltz, A.M., Blakemore, J.E.O. & Berenbaum, S.A. (2013). Sex Differences in Brain and Behavioral Development. *Neural Circuit Development and Function in the Brain, Comprehensive Developmental Neuroscience*. Philadelphia: Academic Press.

Carnes, P.J. (1997). *Sexual Anorexia, Overcoming Sexual Self-Hatred*. Center City, Minnesota: Hazelden.

Cavanagh Johnson, T. (2013). *Updated Understanding Children's Sexual Behaviors, What's Natural and Healthy*. San Diego: Family Violence and Sexual Assault Institute.

Coie, J. D. & Jacobs, M. R. (1993). The role of social context in the prevention of conduct disorder. *Development and Psychopathology, 5*, 263–275.

Davis, L. (1990). *The Courage to Heal Workbook, For Men and Women Survivors of Child Sexual Abuse*. Harper Collins: New York.

Dreger, A.D. (1998). Ambiguous Sex' or Ambivalent Medicine? Ethical Issues in the Treatment of Intersexuality, *Hastings Center Report 28(3)*, 24-36.

Dreger, A.D. (2011). Is Anatomy Destiny? TED talks. http://www.ted.com/talks/alice_dreger_is_anatomy_destiny.html

Edelman, B. (2009) Red Light States: Who buys online adult entertainment. *Journal of Economic Perspectives — Volume 23, Number 1 — Winter 2009 — Pages 209–220.*

Else-Quest, N.M., Hyde, J.S., Goldsmith, H.H. & Van Hulle, C.A. (2006). Gender differences in temperament: A meta-analysis. *Psychological Bulletin, Vol. 132*(1), 33-72.

Hadsall, C. (2010). Characteristics of Sexually Healthy Adults. Minnesota Department of Health. www.health.state.mn.us/topics/sexualhealth/characteristics.pdf

Ingalhalikar, M., Smith, A., Parker, D., Satterthwaite, T.D., Elliott, M.A., Ruparel, K., Hakonarson, H., Gur, R.E., Gur, R.C. & Verma, R. (2013).
Sex differences in the structural connectome of the human brain. Proceedings of the National Academy of Sciences.

Farkas, R.H., Unger, E.F. & Temple, R. (2013). Zolpidem and Driving impairment — Identifying Persons at Risk. *New England Journal of Medicine, 369,* 689-691.

Finkelhor, D. & Browne, A. (1985). The Traumatic Impact of Child Sexual Abuse: A Conceptualization. *American Journal of Orthopsychiatry, 55*(4).

Friedrich, W. & Chaffin, M. (2000). *Developmental-systematic perspectives on children and sexual behavior problems.* San Diego, CA: Association for the Treatment of Sexual Abusers.

Friedrich, W. (2002). Child sexual behavior inventory: normative, psychiatric and sexual abuse comparisons. *Child Maltreatment, 6*(1), 37-49.

Hindman, J. (1985). *A Very Touching Book: For Little People and For Big People (2nd Ed.).* Ontario, OR: AlexAndria Associates.

Hindman, J. (2006). *There is No Sex Fairy To Protect Our Children from Becoming Sexual Abusers.* Lincoln City, OR: AlexAndria Associates.

Johnson, T.C. (1998). Children who molest. In W. Marshall, S. Hudson, T. Ward, & Y. Fernandex (Eds.), *Sourcebook of treatment programs for sexual offenders.* New York: Plenum.

Kendall-Tackett, K.A., Williams, L. & Finkelhor, D. (1993). Impact of sexual abuse on children: A review and synthesis of recent empirical studies. *Psychological Bulletin, 113*(1), 164-180.

Maltz, W. (2001). *The Sexual Healing Journey: A Guide for Survivors of Sexual Abuse (Revised Edition).* William Morrow: New York.

Maltz, W. (2014). Part I Understanding, What is Healthy Sex? Healthy Sex.com

Mendle, J., Leve, L.D., Van Ryzin, M. & Natsuaki, M.N. (2013). Linking childhood maltreatment with girls' internalizing symptoms: early puberty as a tipping point. *Journal of Research on Adolescents, 23*(4).

Merriam-Webster. (2014). http://www.merriam-webster.com/dictionary.

Mischel, W. Ebbesen, E.B. & Zeiss A.B. (1972). "Cognitive and attentional mechanisms in delay of gratification." *Journal of Personality and Social Psychology* 21(2), 204–218.

Money, J. & Ehrhardt, A. (1996). *Man & Woman, Boy & Girl: Gender Identity from Conception to Maturity*. Northvale, N.J.: Jason Aronson.

Steinmetz, K. (2014). America's Transition. *Time Vol. 183*(22), 38-46.

Underwood, M. K., Moore, B., & Galperin, M. (2002). Gender differences in friendship exclusivity and social aggression: Evidence from observations and questionnaires. In L. Zarbatany, M. Underwood, & H. M. Trautner (Chairs), Gender and friendship: Evidence of two worlds? Symposium presented at the 17th Biennial Meeting of the International Society for the Study of Social and Behavioral Development, Ottawa, Canada.

Widom, C & Ames, M. (1994). Criminal consequences of childhood sexual victimization. *Child Abuse and Neglect, 18*(4), 303-318.

World Health Organization. (2006). "Defining sexual health: report of a technical consultation on sexual health." Geneva, World Health Organization.
http://www.who.int/reproductive-
health/publications/sexualhealth/
index.html.

World Health Organization. (2010). "Measuring sexual health: Conceptual and practical considerations and related indicators." Switzerland.

Ziegler, D.L. (1987). "Inappropriate Sexual Behavior Scale," Monograph of The Assessment and Treatment of Sexual Abusers conference of the Association for the Behavioral Treatment of Sexual Abusers, Portland OR.

Ziegler, D. (2008). Promoting Healthy Sexuality after Sexual Abuse.
http://www.jaspermountain.org/promoting_healthy_sexuality.pdf.

Ziegler, D.L. (2009). *Beyond Healing: The Path to Personal Contentment after Trauma.* Phoenix: Acacia Publishing.

Ziegler, D.L. (2011). *Traumatic Experience and the Brain, A Handbook for Understanding and Treating Those Traumatized as Children, Second Edition.* Phoenix: Acacia Publishing.

Appendix

Inappropriate Sexual Behavior Scale
Dave Ziegler, Ph.D.

Abstract

In the early 1980's, there was a startling realization that children are often sexually victimized by other children. With this understanding has come a serious confusion as to what constitutes normative sexual expression and what is sexual exploitation. This article discusses the two stances that have been prevalent: 1) discourage or ignore sexual behavior in children and hope that it goes away, or 2) persistent sexual behavior, particularly with other children, is either pathological or a definitive sign of emerging pathology. The disparity and myopic nature of both positions makes them unacceptable. How do we then take a more balanced and accurate view of childhood sexual expression, given our new sensitivity to children exhibiting sexually offending behavior? The Inappropriate Sexual Behavior Scale is presented as a tool to take into consideration normative sexual themes and behavior in children and the possibility of developing sexual pathology:

The Discovery that Children are Sexual Beings

Historically, it is difficult to determine just when the realization occurred that children, as well as adults, are sexual creatures with all the resulting ramifications. From a sociological perspective, it is clear that what our culture still considers part of childhood (11 to 18 years of age) in many cultures would have already undergone the rite of passage to adulthood – work, conscription into the army, leaving home, taking a partner, and freedom to be sexually active. Presently, in third-world nations, large percentages of their armed forces

155

are younger than the legal age to view R-rated movies in the United States. It is ironic to the point of absurdity what children in our culture are exposed to, concerning sexuality and the restrictions we place on their response to this exposure. Television, movies, magazines and even comic books frequently depict mild-to-strong sexual themes such as nudity, sexual suggestiveness, sexual behavior and sexualized dominance and violence. Yet about the only culturally agreed upon sexual behavior of children is to ask a biology question or two. When it comes to sexuality, the disparity between the physical or hormonal clock and the cultural clock exacerbates the difficulty.

But even with younger children under eleven, the presence of sexual themes and issues was given credible scrutiny by Freud. In theory at least all human beings have sexual feelings, drives and motivations including children.

Pushing Sex Underground

With an emerging complex society, the age of maturation has been driven higher and higher. For adults over fifty, it was not unusual that children of twelve contribute to the family income in the 1940's and 1950's. Child labor laws and other mechanistic changes have pushed children out of the work force and further from the rites of passage to adulthood. The puritan answer to young people ready to experience sexual expression, but considered by the culture as too young, was a rigid good-and-evil construct. Sexual behaviors, and even sexual thoughts, were wrong and punishable by possible insanity here and eternal damnation in the hereafter; while abstinence was virtue with rewards one-hundred-fold – later on. This state of affairs has produced a cultural protocol to punish sexual behavior and to ignore sexuality in children with the hope that it will somehow go away.

While the prevailing strategy is still to pretend that children are not sexual beings, the inescapable fact is that the average first-grader witnesses more sexual behavior in a year of viewing prime-time television than Sigmund Freud dealt with in his career. The most that can be said about our culture's position on sexuality is that we know it isn't working – teenage pregnancies and adolescent sexual offenders are two of the many indicators of this.

Our Eyes are Opened to Sexual Abuse

Twenty years ago, few professionals questioned the presence of sexual abuse among children and as a 1975 psychiatrist text stated, it could be found in one in every million homes (Kohn, 1987). In the last twenty years, we have come to realize that sexual abuse may be in one in every four-to-ten homes. A more recent realization is that sexual abuse is often perpetrated by another child. Children's sex games are no longer viewed with attitudes like "boys will be boys" or "they are only kids." In the state of Oregon during 1985, over 1,000 arrests of children under the age of 18 were made for sexual offenses. A surprise finding was that the majority of children arrested for sex crimes were under the age of 14 (1).

National media has helped our society understand the prevalence of sexual abuse. Stories abound of the school teachers, police officers and ministers who have lived a secret life of harming children. It is now clear that for incarcerated pedophiles, their disturbance began to manifest in their early teens. "Sex play" can no longer be ignored or merely punished and pushed underground. It must be exposed, understood, and effectively responded to.

But, in our new awareness of sexual pathology, the pendulum has swung to the dark side. In the last three years, sexual expression by children is being treated and referred to by many professionals as pathological or pre-pathological. Certainly, our culture has learned that children are sexual beings and will present sexual themes and behaviors which are normative by definition and not signs of disturbance. Understanding sexual expression has now become extremely difficult.

The Inappropriate Sexual Behavior Scale

The challenge that faces us is to sift through the complex continuum of normative behavior to sexually exploitive abuse. The following Scale is a tool to help with the analysis of childhood sexual expression:

1	2	3	4	5
Sexualized Expression	Cooperative Sexualized Expression	Emotional Abuse of Sexual Nature	Emotionally Coercive Sexual Abuse	Physically Coercive Sexual Abuse
Sex writing Sex drawing "Dirty" talk Masturbation Childish sex calls	**Mutually consenting sex games/ Curious exploration**	**Exhibitionism Voyeurism Obscene calls Frottage**	**Premeditated genital contact with Narcissism Manipulation Thinking errors**	**Forcible Demeaning And/or brutal Sexual contact**

Not all the behaviors in the first two categories are necessarily inappropriate in themselves. However, for this Scale it is understood that the mentioned behaviors have become problematic in a specific setting. The Scale allows any inappropriate sexual behavior to appear somewhere on the point scale. The higher the point scale the more serious the behavior and the greater the potential or presence of pathology. Point scores of 3.5 and higher indicate issues best treated in the context of a specific sex offender program (3.5 would indicate behaviors in this category that are frequent or habitual). Scores above 3.0 are reportable to police agencies as delinquent sexual behavior. Scores above 4.0 are reportable to the proper authorities as sexual abuse.

To best understand the categories within the scale. It is important to recognize that each has corresponding behaviors and attitudes. The same behaviors can have a completely different quality depending upon the attitude behind it. In the following list the behaviors and attitudes are neither all-inclusive nor will all attitudinal states necessarily be present.

Category	Attitudes	Behaviors
1 **Sexualized Expression**	*Unsophisticated* *Curious* *Naïve* *Spontaneous* *Explorative* *Fascinated* *Scared/excited*	*Masturbation* *Sexual graffiti* *Sexual notes* *Sexual "dirty talk"* *Sexual phone calls* *Looking at underwear ads* *Staring at body parts*
2 **Cooperative Sexualized Expression**	*Impulsive* *Inquisitive* *Opportunistic* *Curious* *Mutuality* *Secretive* *Consenting* *Experimentation*	*Sex games* *Mutual touching* *Visual exploration* *Observing eliminations* *Sexual mimicry of adults* *Generalized sex play*
3 **Emotionally Coercive Sexual Abuse**	*Anxious* *Fixated* *Lacking self-control* *Obsessive* *Preoccupied* *Prurient interest* *Premeditation* *Isolation*	*Exhibitionism* *Frottage* *Voyeurism* *Sexual harassment* *Fetish theft* *Obscene phone calls*
4 **Physically Coercive Sexual Abuse**	*Narcissism* *Premeditation* *Manipulation/trickery* *Lacks remorse* *Thinking errors*	*Genital contact that is:* *Chronic/progressive* *Progressively intrusive* *Threatening words or acts* *Exploitative* *Multiple victims*

5	Antisocial	Genital contact that is:
Physically Coercive Sexual Abuse	Domination Generalized anger Character disorder Poor impulse control Psycho social-dysfunction	Aggressive Demeaning/humiliating Violent Use of weapon Causing injury Nonsexual serious antisocial behavior

Attitudes and Behaviors

As with all problematic behavior, inappropriate sexual behavior in children needs attention. The type of attention depends upon the facts of the incident. The who, what, when and why of the situation must be carefully considered. It is critical to identify early signs of a developing sexual disorder, particularly potential sexually offending attitudes and behaviors. The population of sexually abused children is a significant group to watch.

Although the Inappropriate Sexual Behavior Scale can be a useful tool in understanding a specific sexual incident or pattern of incidents, it is not in itself a predictor of future sexual behavior. However, the earlier sexual pathology is identified, the better the chance of successful treatment. Of equal importance is not attempting to 'desexualize' children. To respond in punitive or even corrective interventions to normative sexual themes and behaviors gives an unhealthy message to children about sex particularly those with moderate-to-severe distortions to begin with (resulting from abuse). Treating sexual abuse victims requires identification and treatment of pathology, as well as an environment with sensitivity and understanding of normative sexual expression. Controlling behavior is not a sufficient long-term justification for further distortions of the healthy role of sexuality in growing up. In treating sexually abused children, great care must be taken to re-socialize healthy viewpoints while avoiding new, however subtle, distorted messages concerning sexuality.

References

Alfie Kohn, "Shattered Innocences", <u>Psychology Today</u>, 2/87.

(1) Avalon Associates, <u>The Oregon Report on Juvenile Sexual Offenders</u>, Salem, Oregon: Department of Human Resources, 1986.

Michael O'Brien and Walter Bera, "Adolescent Sexual Offenders: A Descriptive Typology", <u>Preventing Sexual Abuse</u>, Fall 1986.

Gary A. Wenet and Toni F. Clark, "Juvenile Sexual Offender Decision Criteria", University of Washington.

Dave Ziegler, "Childhood Sexual Behavior In Residential Care", Jasper Mountain 1987.